RECORDED VERSIONS
GUITAR

AUTHENTIC TRANSCRIPTIONS
WITH NOTES AND TABLATURE

ROCK BAND 2 ™

ISBN 978-1-4234-6229-3

HAL•LEONARD® CORPORATION

7777 W. BLUEMOUND RD. P.O. BOX 13819 MILWAUKEE, WI 53213

Visit Hal Leonard Online at
www.halleonard.com

CONTENTS

Alive

Music by Stone Gossard
Lyric by Eddie Vedder

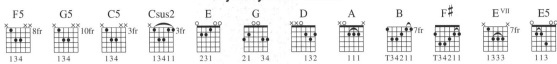

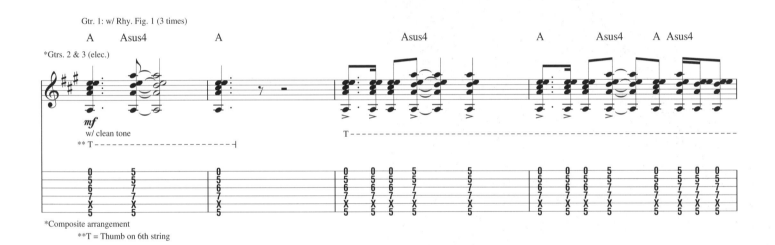

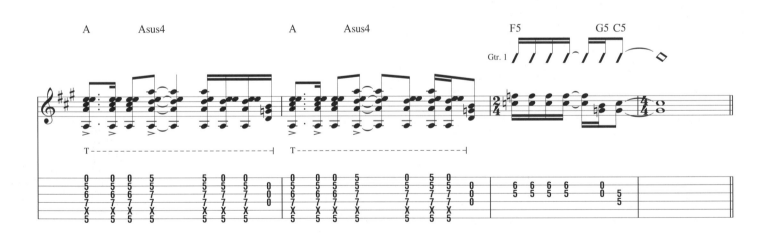

*Composite arrangement

**T = Thumb on 6th string

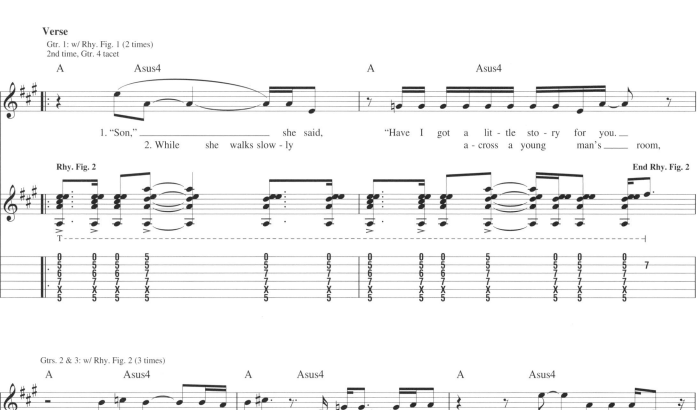

Verse

Gtr. 1: w/ Rhy. Fig. 1 (2 times)
2nd time, Gtr. 4 tacet

1. "Son," _____ she said, "Have I got a lit-tle sto-ry for you. __
2. While she walks slow-ly a-cross a young man's ____ room,

Rhy. Fig. 2   End Rhy. Fig. 2

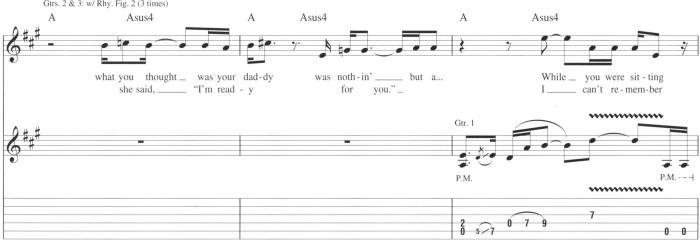

Gtrs. 2 & 3: w/ Rhy. Fig. 2 (3 times)

what you thought __ was your dad-dy was noth-in' ____ but a...   While __ you were sit-ting
she said, ____ "I'm read-y for you." __   I ____ can't re-mem-ber

Gtr. 1

P.M.   P.M. - - - ┐

Gtr. 1: w/ Rhy. Fig. 1 (2nd meas.)   Gtr. 1: w/ Rhy. Fig. 1

home a-lone __ at age __ thir-teen,   your real dad-dy was dy - ing;   Sor-ry you did-n't
an-y-thing __ to this __ ver-y day,   'cept the love, __ the love. _____   Oh, __

F5   G5 C5   F5   G5 C5   Csus2

Gtr. 1

(cont. in notation)

see him. __   But I'm ____ glad _____ we talked." __   Oh, _____
____ you know where,   now I ____ can see. _____   I just __

Gtrs. 2 & 3

(cont. in slashes)

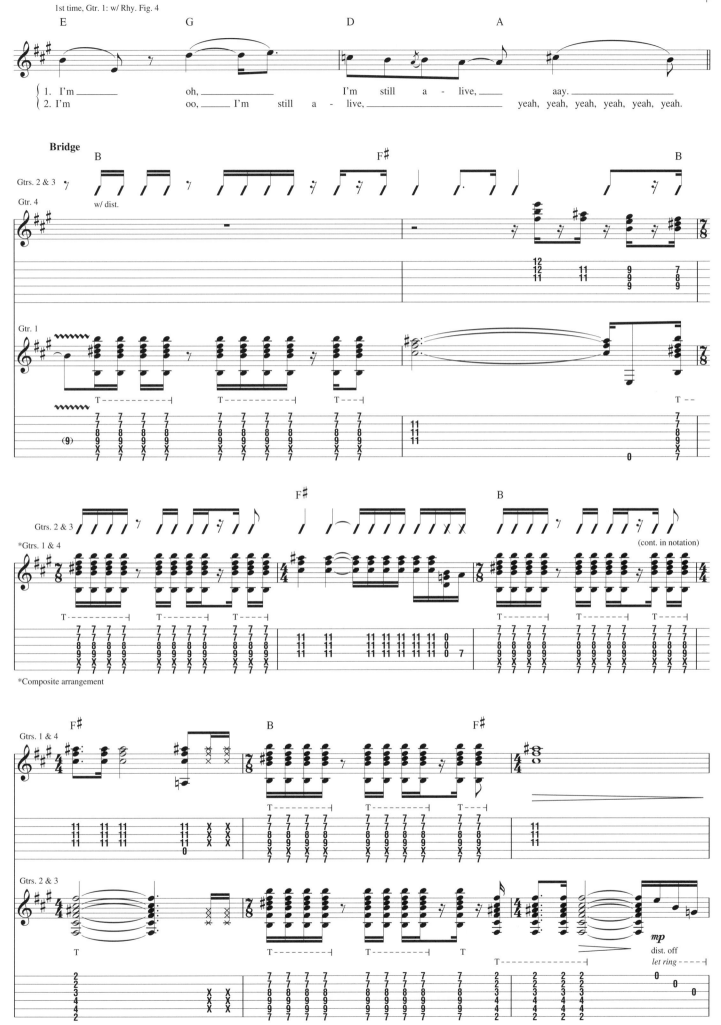

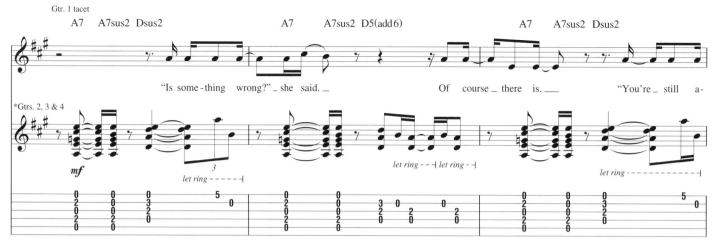

Gtr. 1 tacet

A7 A7sus2 Dsus2   A7 A7sus2 D5(add6)   A7 A7sus2 Dsus2

"Is some-thing wrong?" _ she said. _   Of course _ there is. _   "You're _ still a-

*Gtrs. 2, 3 & 4

mf

let ring — let ring —   *let ring — — — — —*

let ring — — — — —

*Composite arrangement

A7 A7sus2 D5(add6)   B7 B7sus2 Esus2   B7 B7sus2 E6sus2

live," she said. _____ Oh, and do I de-serve _ to be? _   Is that the ques-tion?   And if so, _

let ring — — — — —

D.S. al Coda
(take 1st lyrics)

B7 B7sus2 Esus2   E VII

Gtr. 1

_____ if so, _____ who an - swers? Who an - swers? _____

*w/ dist.

(cont. in slashes)

*Gtrs. 2 & 3

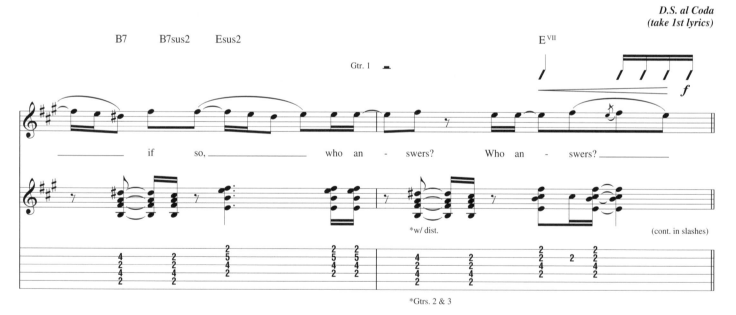

⊕ **Coda**

Guitar Solo

Gtr. 1: w/ Rhy. Fig. 5 (4 times)
Gtrs. 3 & 4: w/ Rhy. Fig. 3A (17 1/2 times)

E   G   D   A

Gtr. 2

w/ wah-wah

Almost Easy

Words and Music by Matthew Sanders, James Sullivan, Brian Haner, Jr. and Zachary Baker

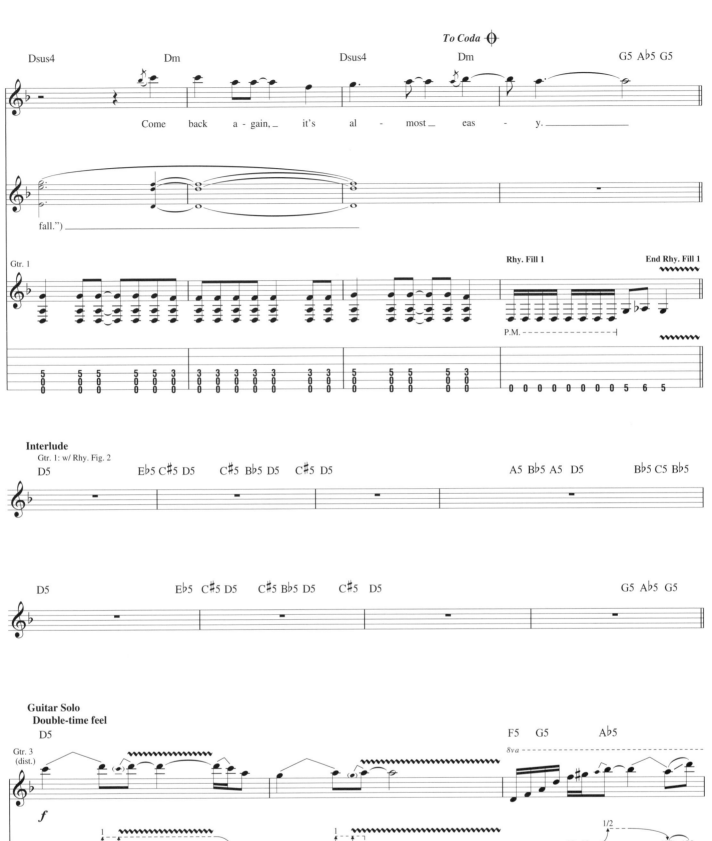
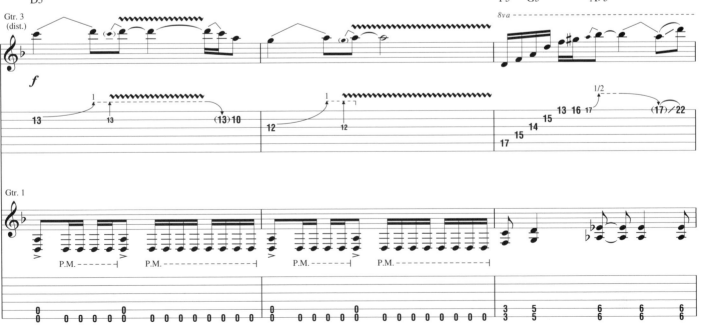

American Woman

Written by Burton Cummings, Randy Bachman, Gary Peterson and Jim Kale

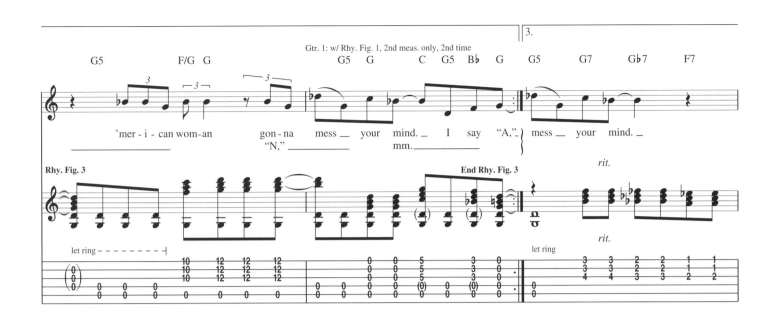

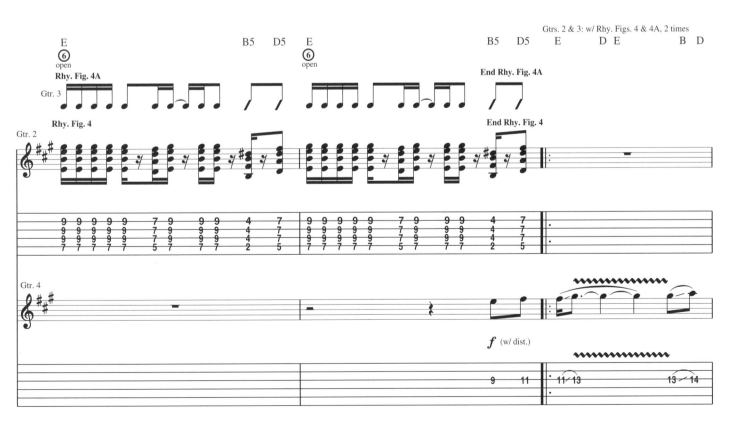

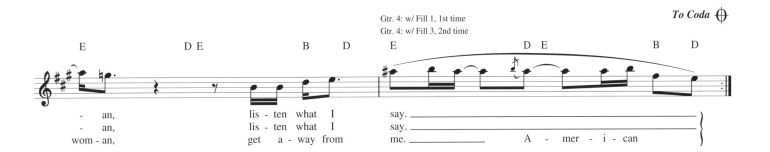

Guitar Solo

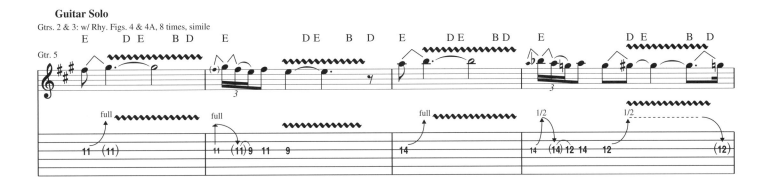

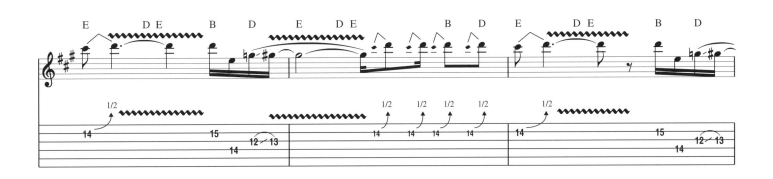

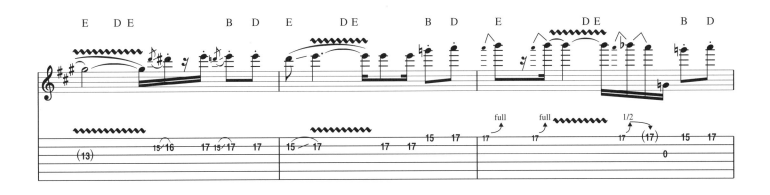

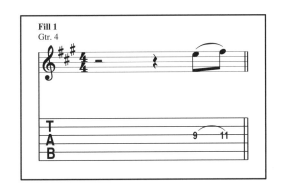

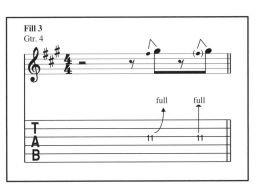

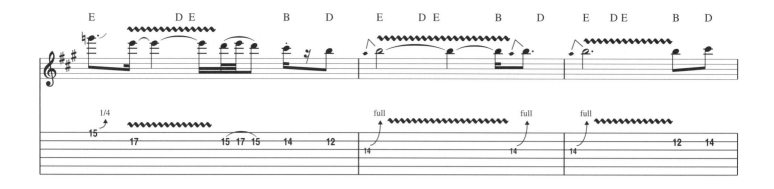

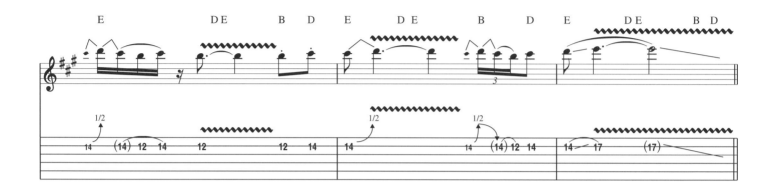

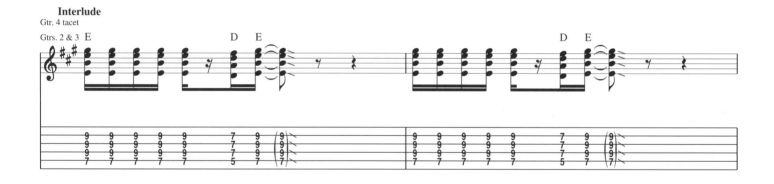

Interlude

Gtr. 4 tacet

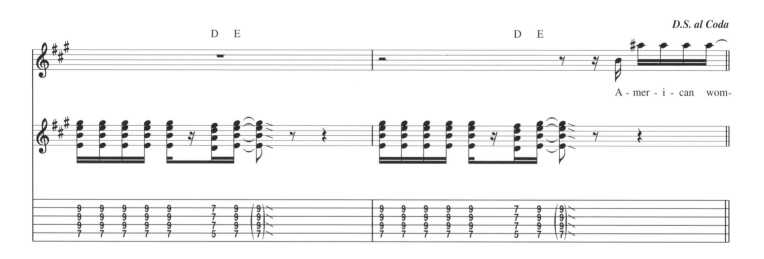

D.S. al Coda

A - mer - i - can wom-

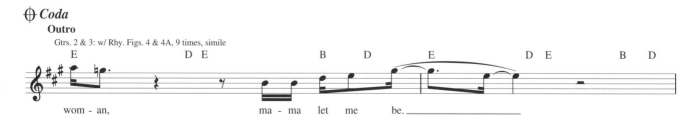

Coda

Outro

Gtrs. 2 & 3: w/ Rhy. Figs. 4 & 4A, 9 times, simile

wom - an, ma - ma let me be. _____

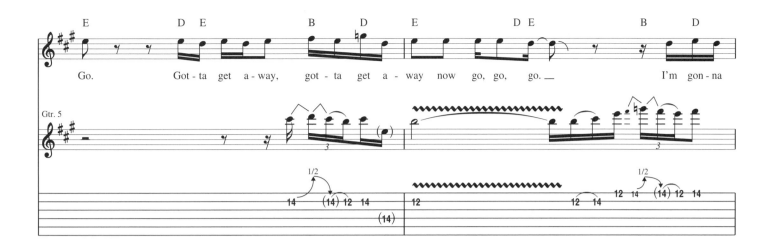

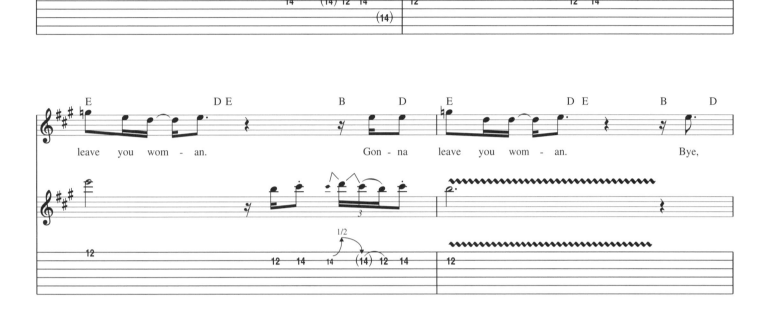

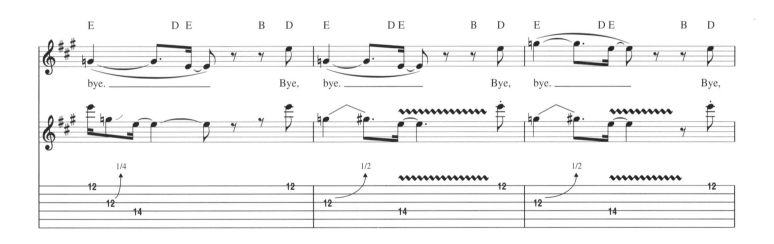

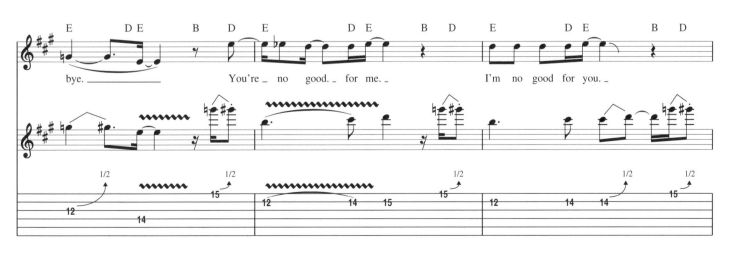

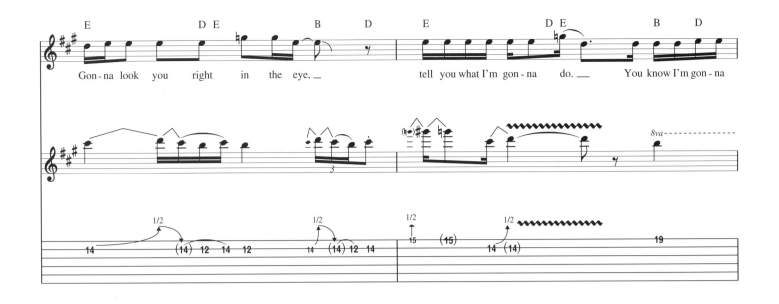

Gon-na look you right in the eye, __ tell you what I'm gon-na do. __ You know I'm gon-na

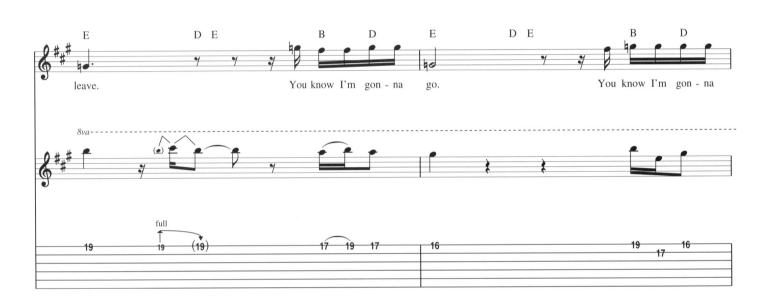

leave. You know I'm gon-na go. You know I'm gon-na

Fade Out

leave. I know I'm gon-na go, _____ wom - an. I'm gon-na...
(ad lib. vocal)

Any Way You Want It

Words and Music by Steve Perry and Neal Schon

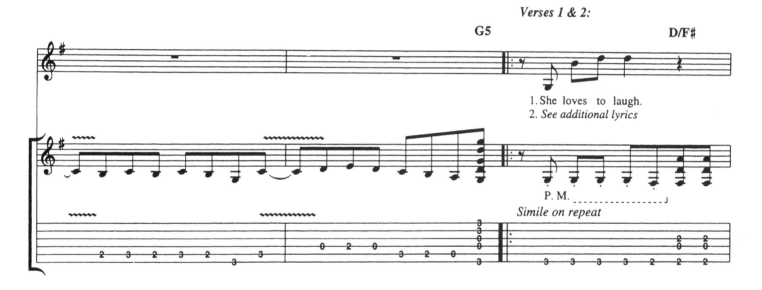

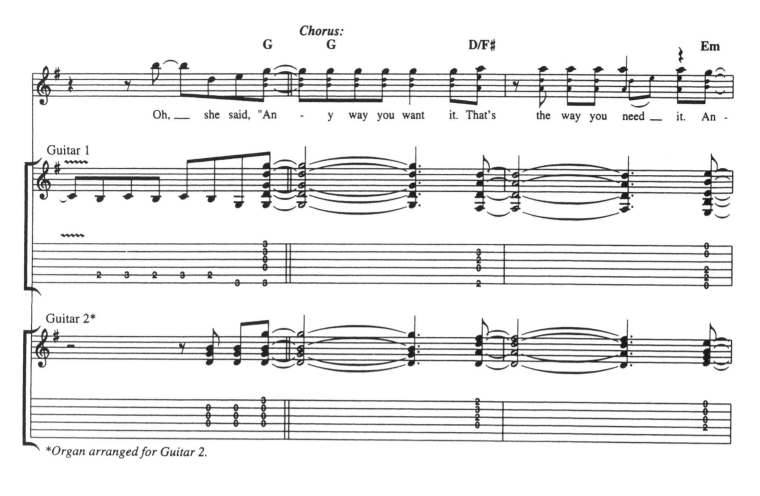

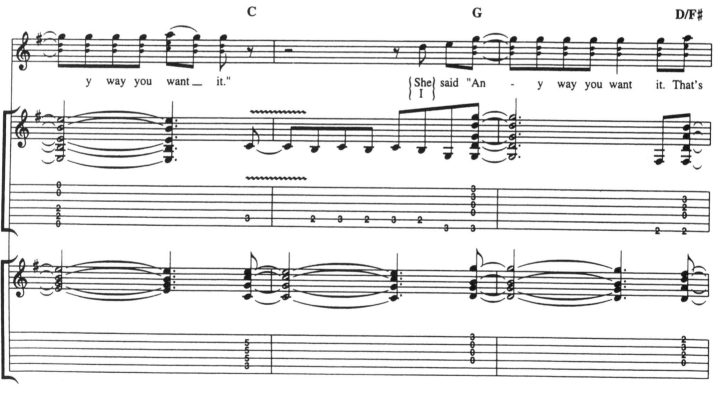

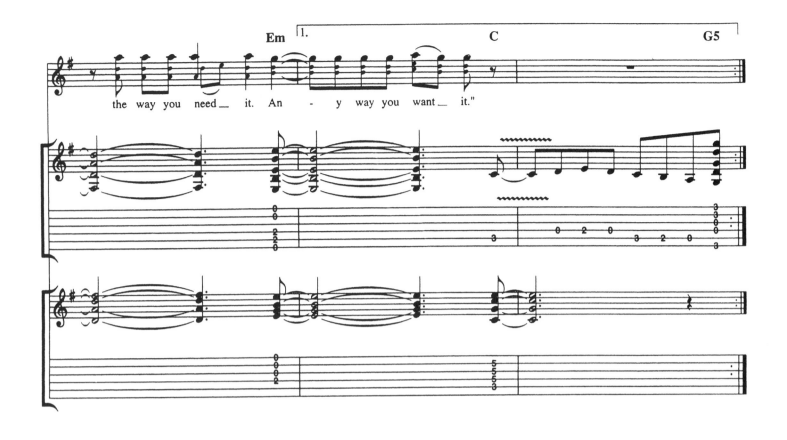

the way you need_ it. An - y way you want_ it."

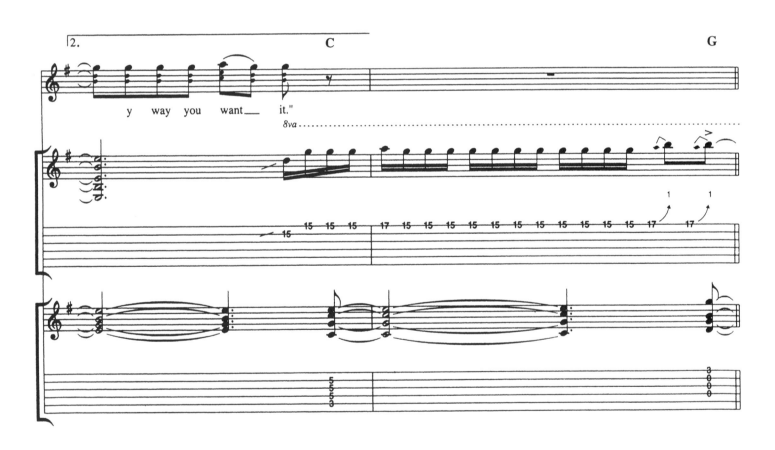

y way you want_ it."

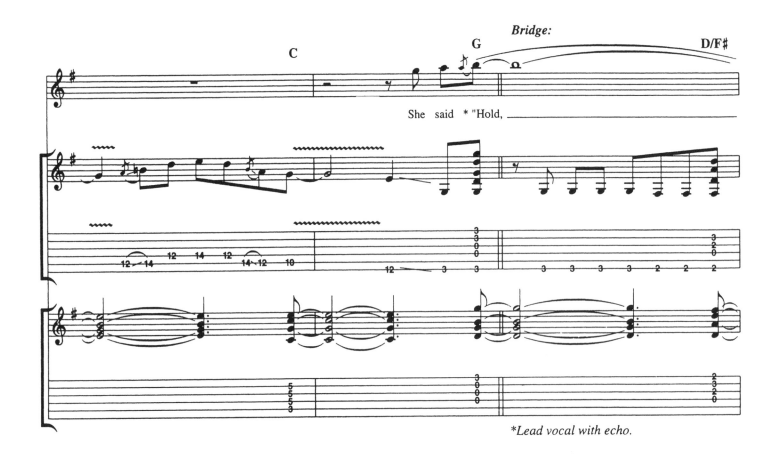

Lead vocal with echo.

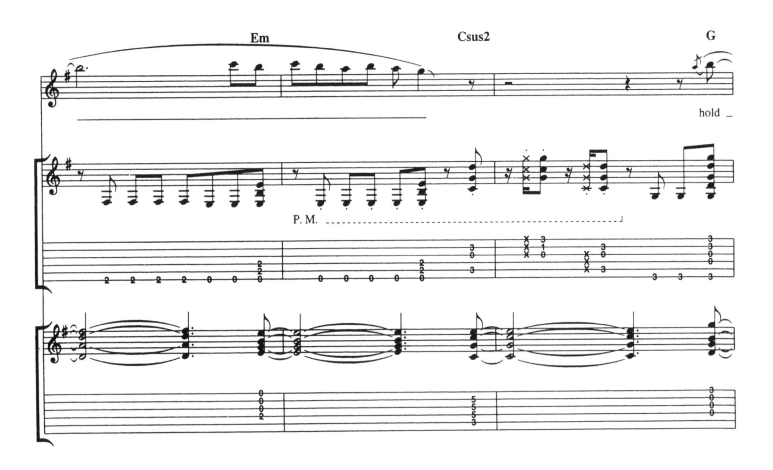

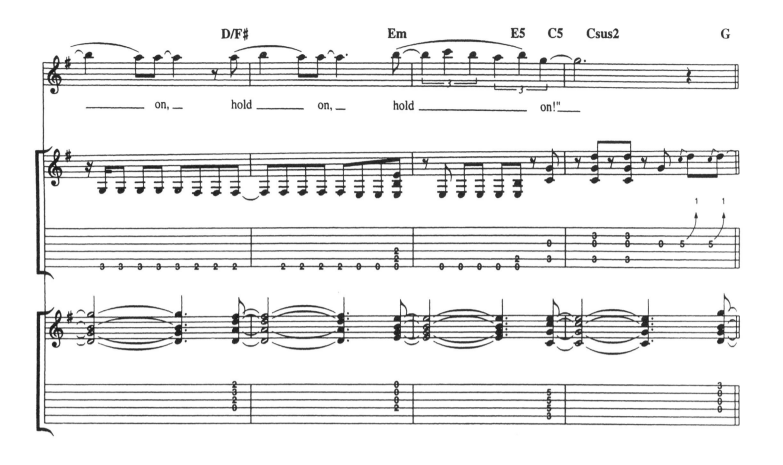

on, ___ hold ___ on, ___ hold _____ on!" ___

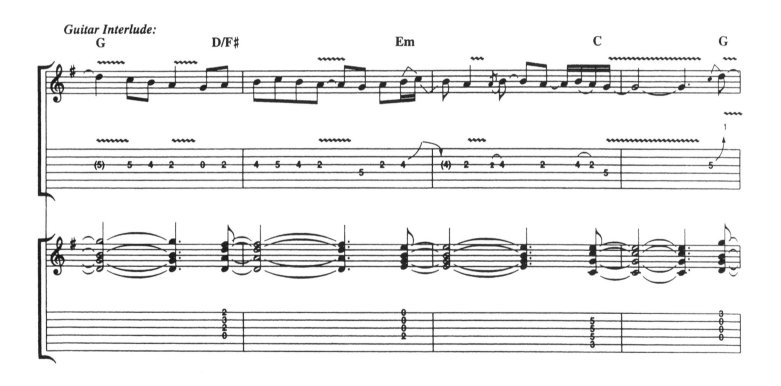

Guitar Interlude:

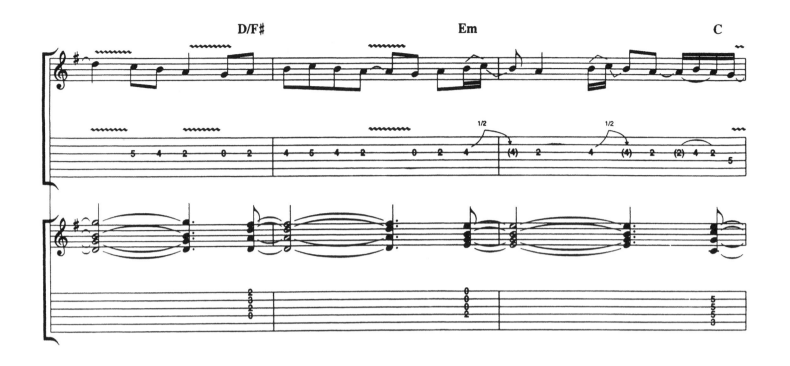

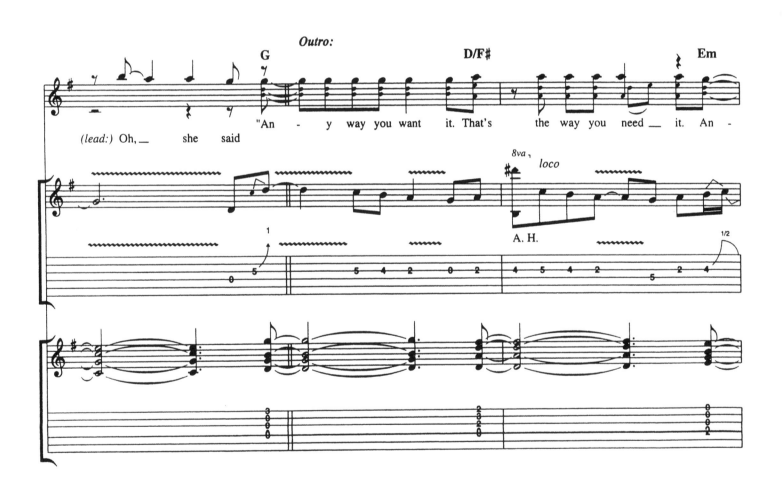

Outro:

(lead:) Oh, __ she said "An - y way you want it. That's the way you need __ it. An -

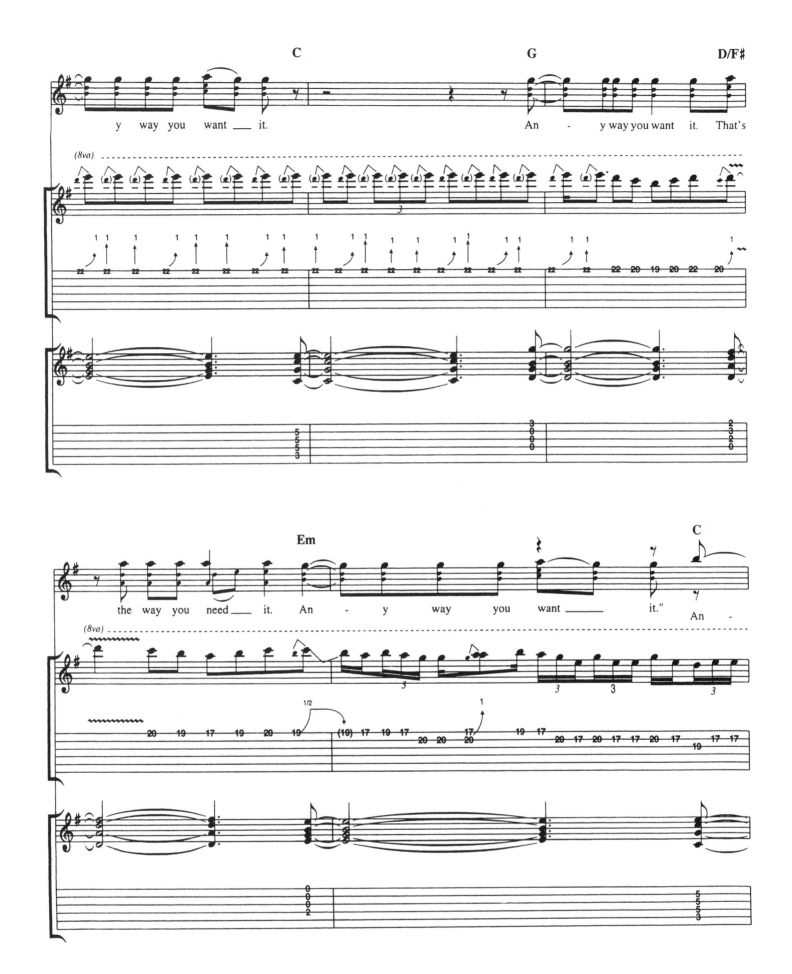

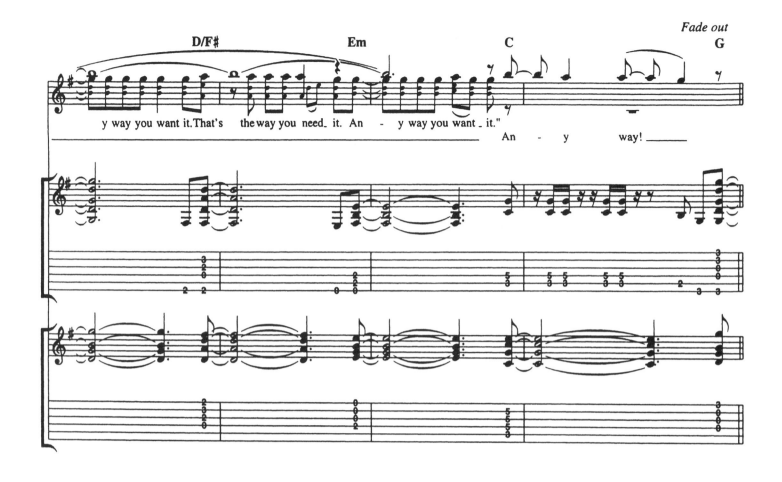

y way you want it. That's the way you need_ it. An — y way you want _ it." An — y way! _____

Additional Lyrics

Verse 2: I was alone,
I never knew
What good love can do.
Ooh, then we touched,
Then we sang,
About the lovin' things.

Ooh, all night, all night,
Oh, every night.
So hold tight, hold tight,
Oh, baby, hold tight.
(To chorus)

Aqualung

Music by Ian Anderson
Lyrics by Jennie Anderson

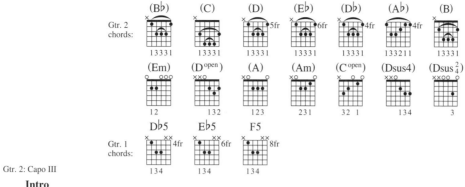

Gtr. 2: Capo III

Intro
Moderately ♩ = 120

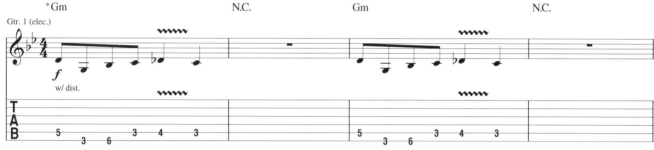

*Chord symbols reflect implied harmony.

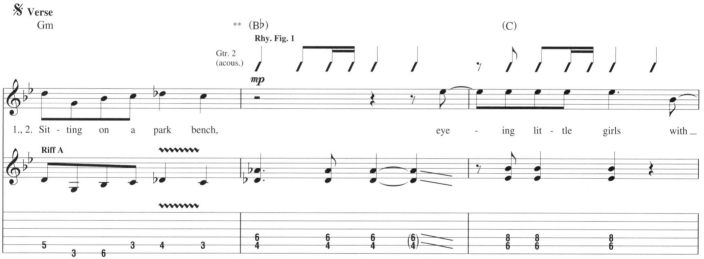

1., 2. Sit-ting on a park bench, eye-ing lit-tle girls with __

**Symbols in parentheses represent chord names respective to capoed guitar and do not reflect actual sounding chords.

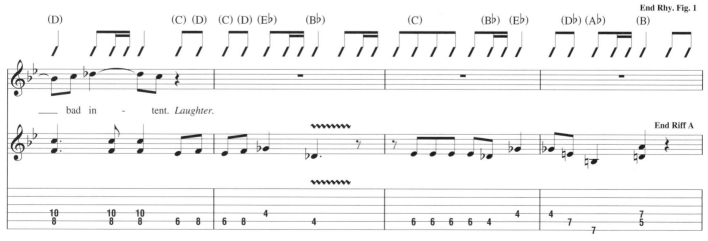

__ bad in - tent. *Laughter.*

*Symbols in parentheses represent chord names respective
to capoed guitar. Symbols above reflect actual sounding chords.

broken ____ luck. ____
{ Oh, ____ } Aq - ua - lung. ____
{ Hey, ____ }

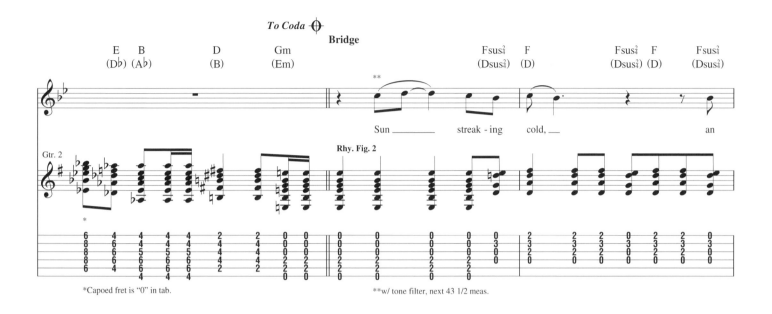

To Coda ⊕

Bridge

Sun ____ streak - ing cold, ____ an

Gtr. 2

Rhy. Fig. 2

*Capoed fret is "0" in tab.
**w/ tone filter, next 43 1/2 meas.

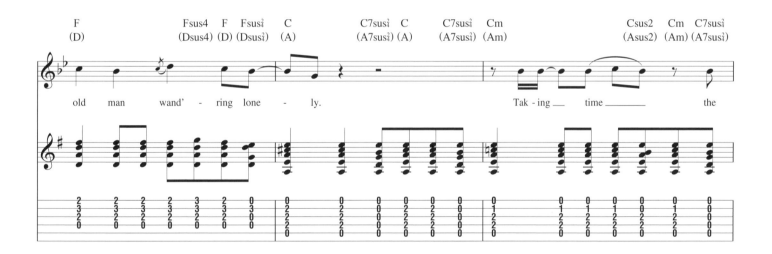

old man wand' - ring lone - ly.
Tak - ing ____ time ____ the

on - ly way ____ he knows. ____

End Rhy. Fig. 2

44

poor old sod, ___ you see it's on - ly me.

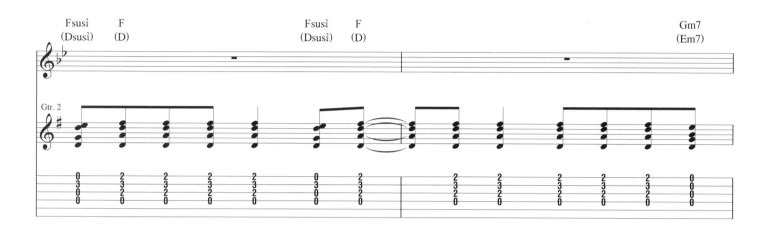

Gtr. 2

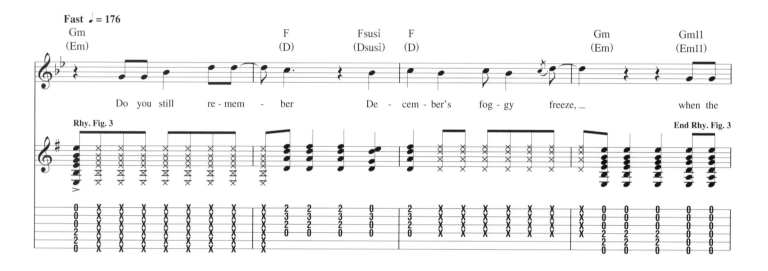

Fast ♩ = 176

Do you still re - mem - ber De - cem - ber's fog - gy freeze, ___ when the

Rhy. Fig. 3

End Rhy. Fig. 3

Gtr. 2: w/ Rhy. Fig. 3

ice that clings ___ on ___ to your beard _____ was scream - ing ag - o - ny? _____ Hey! Then you

*w/ out tone
filter

snatch your rat - tl - ing last ___ breaths with deep sea div - er sounds ___ and the

Gtr. 2

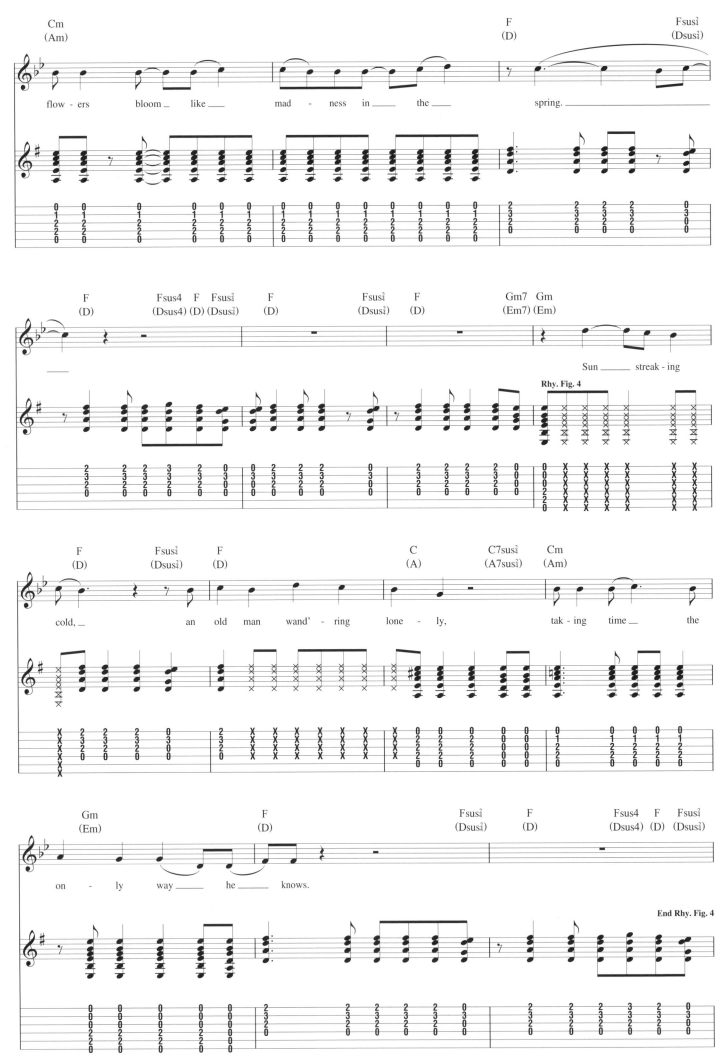

Interlude

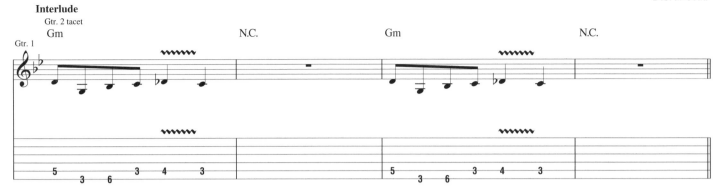

Coda
Outro

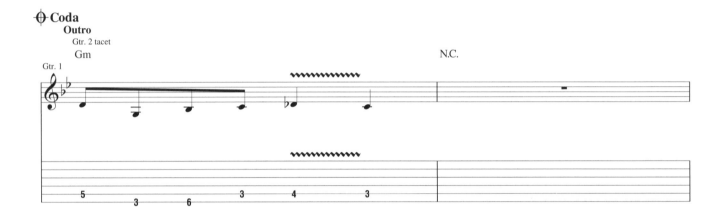

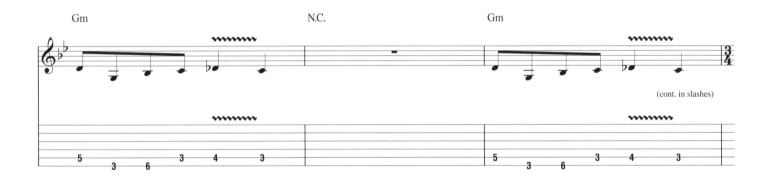

Free time

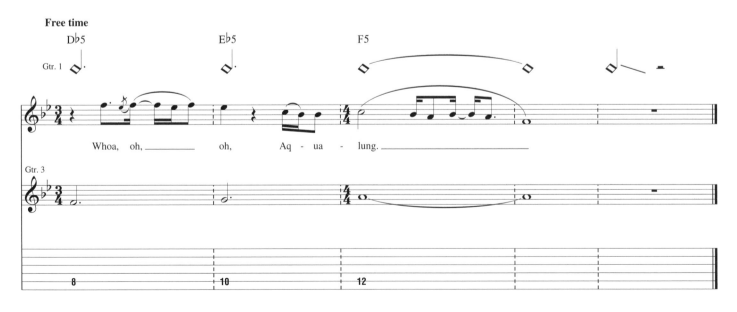

Bodhisattva

Words and Music by Walter Becker and Donald Fagen

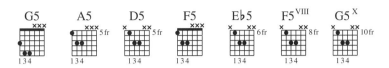

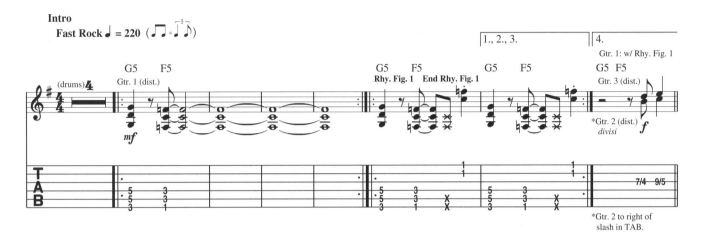

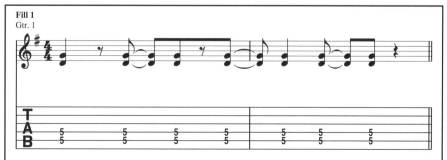

Fill 1
Gtr. 1

**Slide with 1st finger.

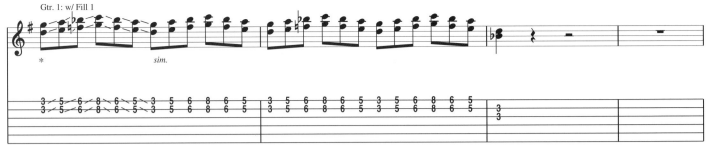

*Barre and slide with 1st finger.

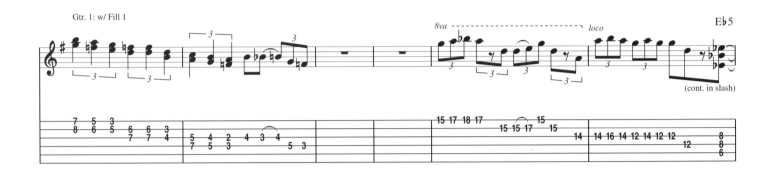

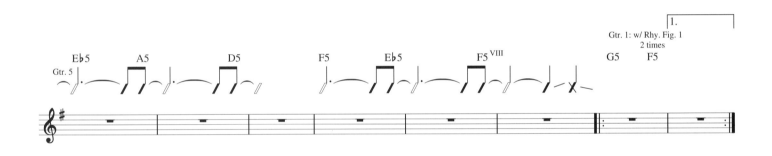

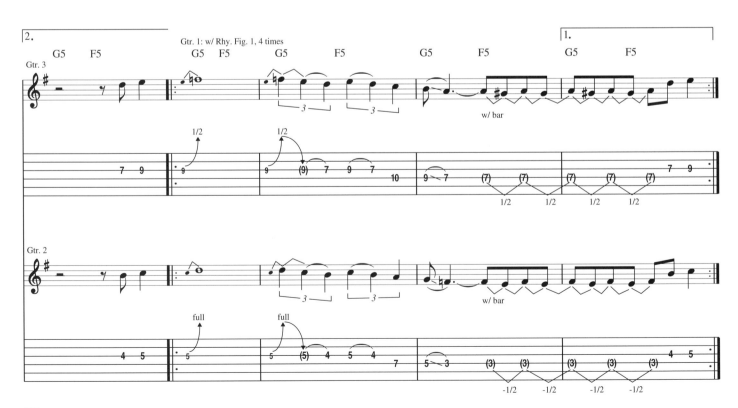

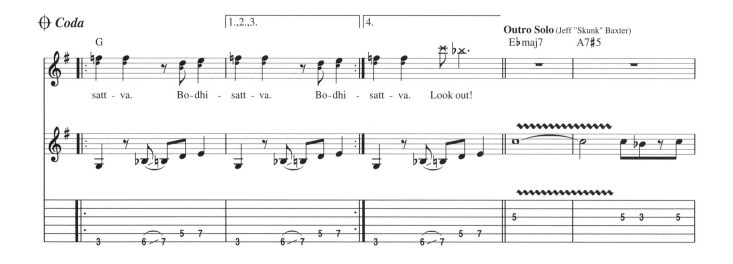

satt - va.   Bo-dhi – satt - va.   Bo-dhi – satt - va.   Look out!

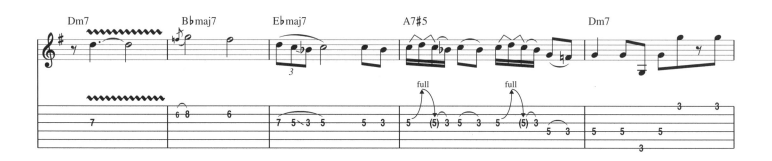

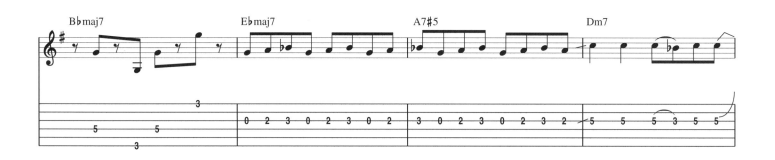

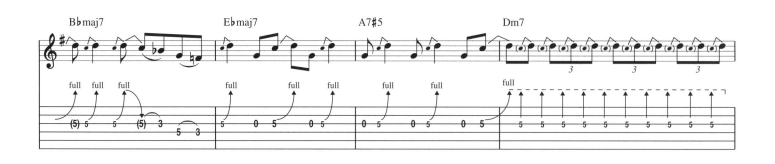

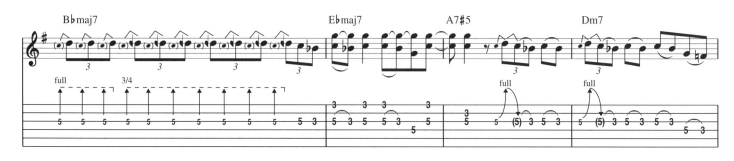

Carry On Wayward Son

Words and Music by Kerry Livgren

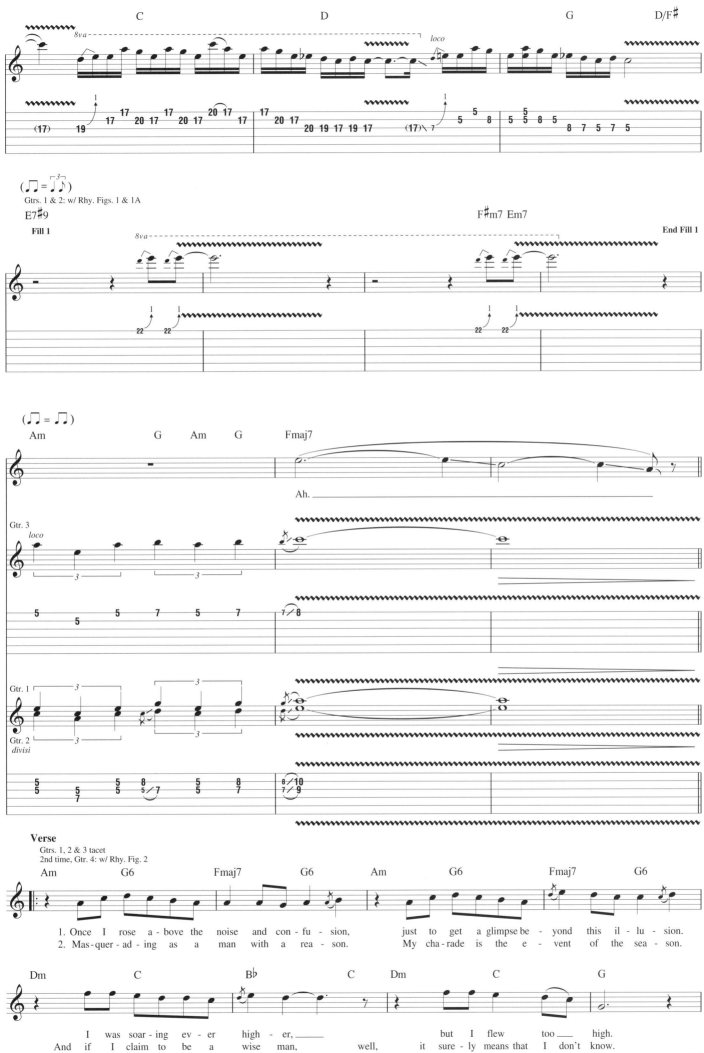

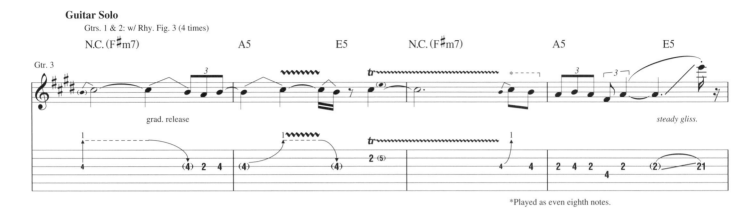

Guitar Solo

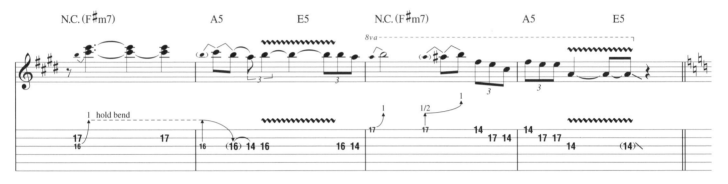

Chop Suey!

Words and Music by Daron Malakian and Serj Tankian

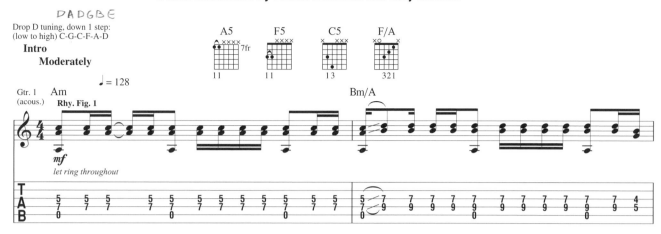

DADGBE

Drop D tuning, down 1 step:
(low to high) C-G-C-F-A-D

Intro
Moderately

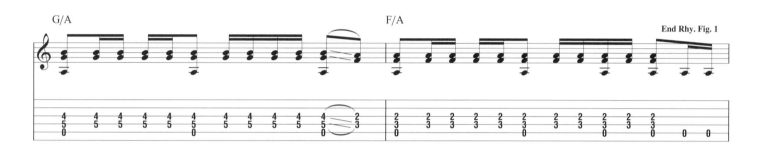

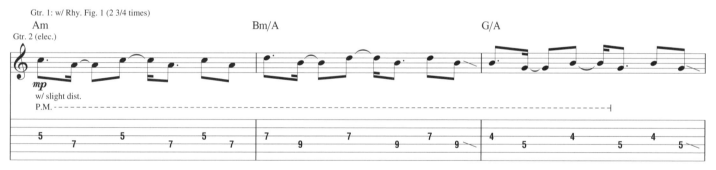

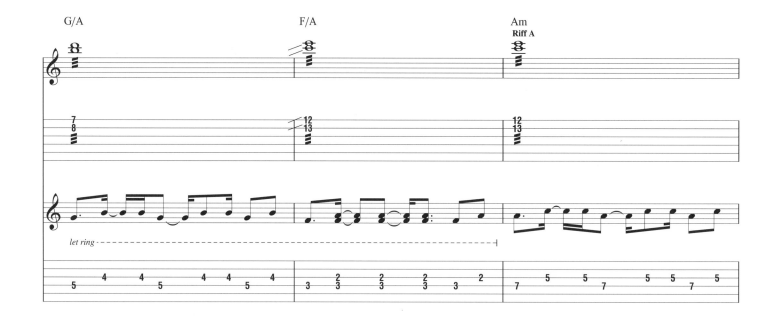

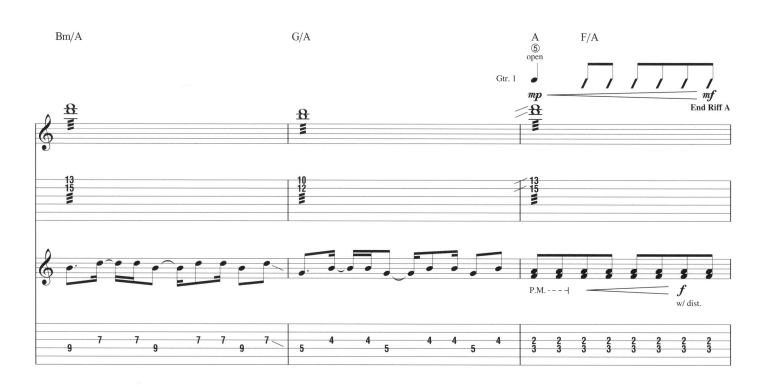

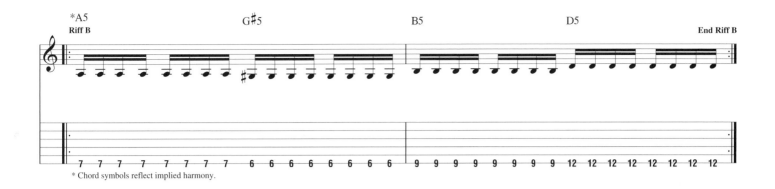

* Chord symbols reflect implied harmony.

Verse

1., 2. Wake up, grab a brush and put a lit-tle make-up. Hide the scars to fade a-way the

Whispered: (Wake up.

Gtr. 4: w/ Rhy. Fig. 3 (3 times)

shake-up. Why'd you leave the keys up-on the ta-ble? Here you go, cre-ate an-oth-er

Hide the scars to fade a-way the...)

fa-ble, you want-ed to. Grab a brush and put a lit-tle make-up, you want-ed to. Hide the scars to fade a-way the

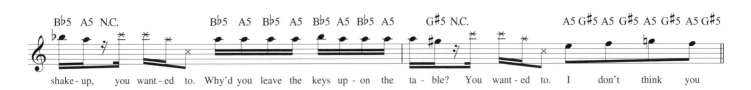

shake-up, you want-ed to. Why'd you leave the keys up-on the ta-ble? You want-ed to. I don't think you

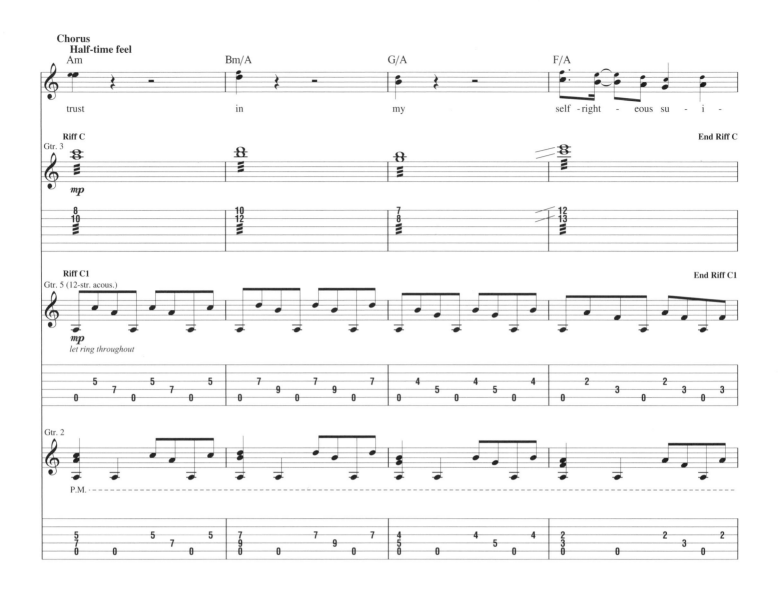

Chorus
Half-time feel

trust in my self-right-eous su-i-

Riff C
Gtr. 3
mp
End Riff C

Riff C1
Gtr. 5 (12-str. acous.)
mp
let ring throughout
End Riff C1

Gtr. 2
P.M.

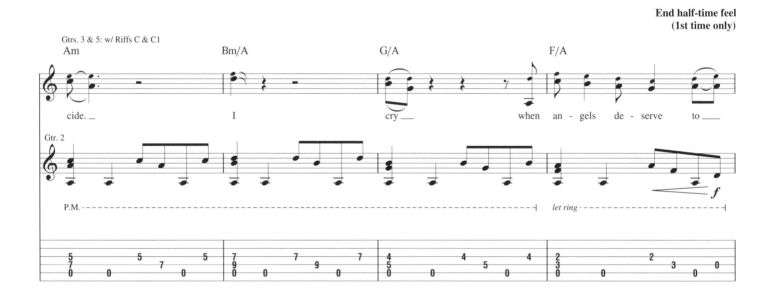

End half-time feel
(1st time only)

Gtrs. 3 & 5: w/ Riffs C & C1

Am   Bm/A   G/A   F/A

cide. ___   I   cry ___   when an-gels de-serve to ___

Gtr. 2
P.M.   *let ring*   *f*

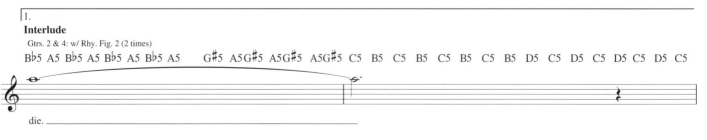

1.

Interlude
Gtrs. 2 & 4: w/ Rhy. Fig. 2 (2 times)

B♭5 A5 B♭5 A5 B♭5 A5 B♭5 A5   G♯5 A5 G♯5 A5 G♯5 A5 G♯5 C5 B5 C5 B5 C5 B5 C5 B5 D5 C5 D5 C5 D5 C5 D5 C5

die. _____

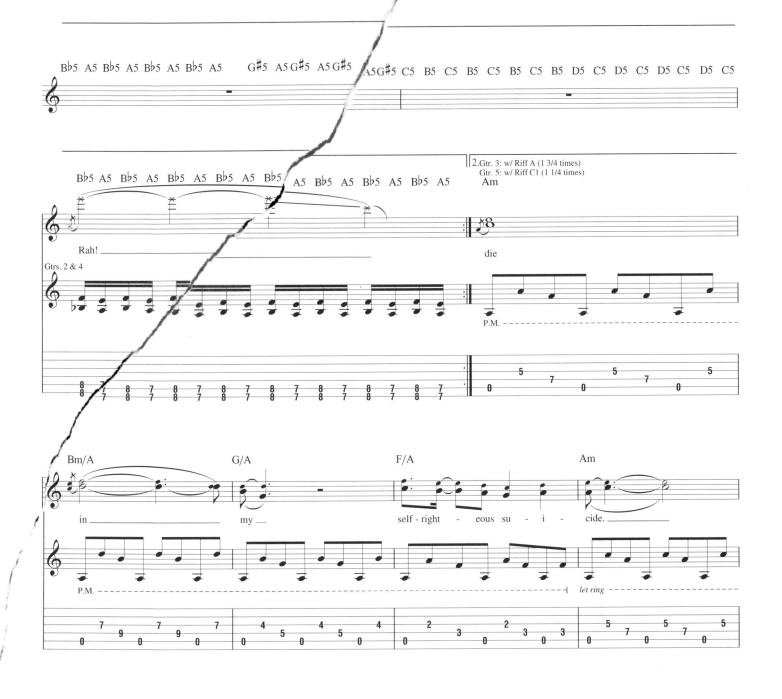

Gtrs. 2 & 4: w/ Rhy. Figs. 4 & 4A (4 3/4 times)
Gtr. 3: w/ Riff D

sak - en — me in your heart? For - sak - en — me. — I'll

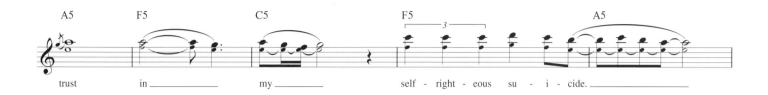

trust in — my — self - right - eous su - i - cide. —

I — cry — when an - gels de - serve to die — in

my — self - right - eous su - i - cide. — I — cry — when

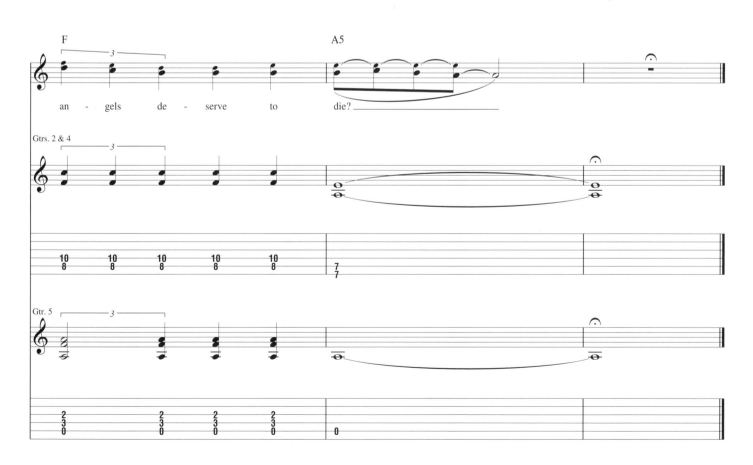

an - gels de - serve to die? —

Come Out and Play

Words and Music by Dexter Holland

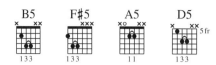

Intro

Moderately Fast Rock ♩ = 158

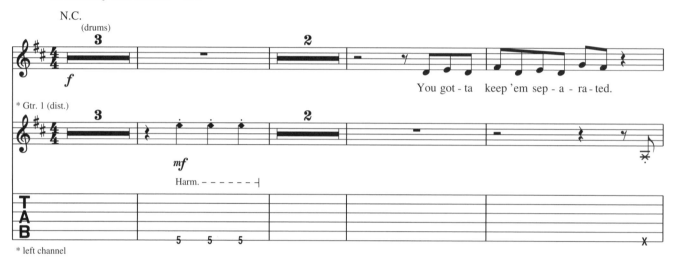

You got-ta keep 'em sep-a-ra-ted.

* Gtr. 1 (dist.)

Harm. - - - - - -|

* left channel

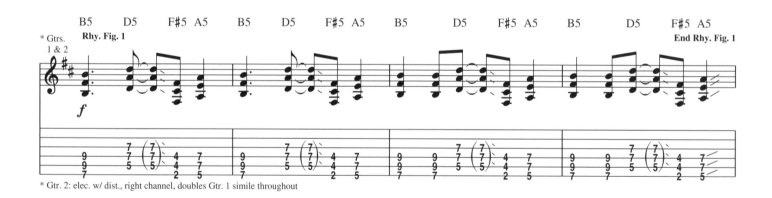

* Gtr. 2: elec. w/ dist., right channel, doubles Gtr. 1 simile throughout

Gtrs. 1 & 2: w/ Rhy. Fig. 1, simile

Gtr. 3 (dist.)

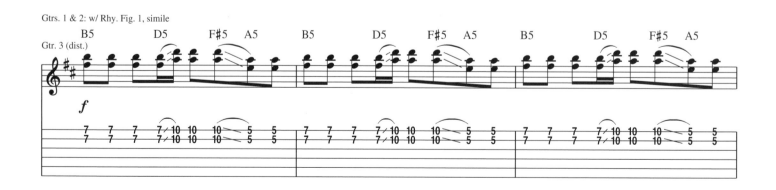

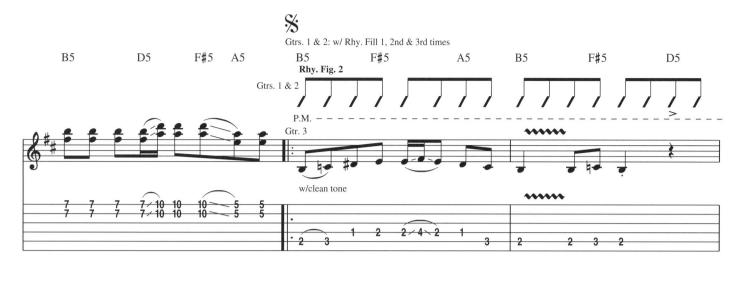

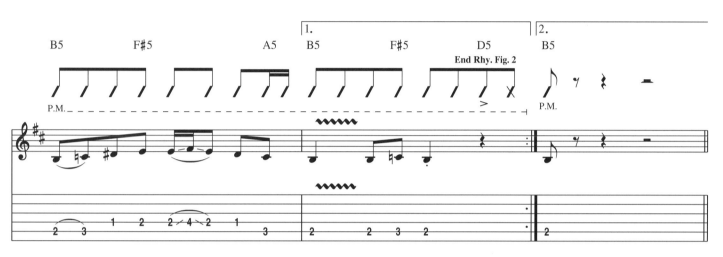

Verse

1. Like the lat-est fash - ion, like a spread-ing dis - ease. _
2. By the time you hear the si - ren it's al - read - y too late.

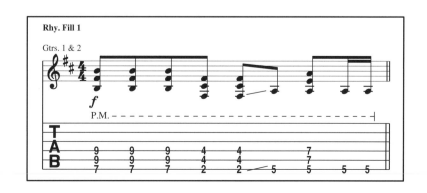

Down with the Sickness

Words and Music by Mike Wengren, Dan Donegan, Dave Draiman and Steve "Fuzz" Kmak

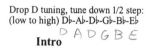

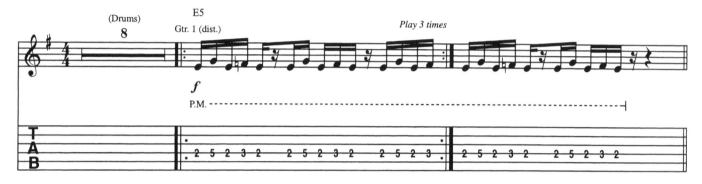

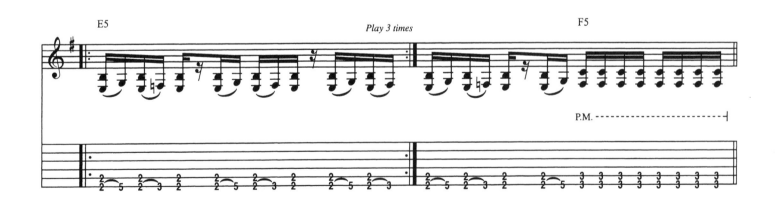

Verse

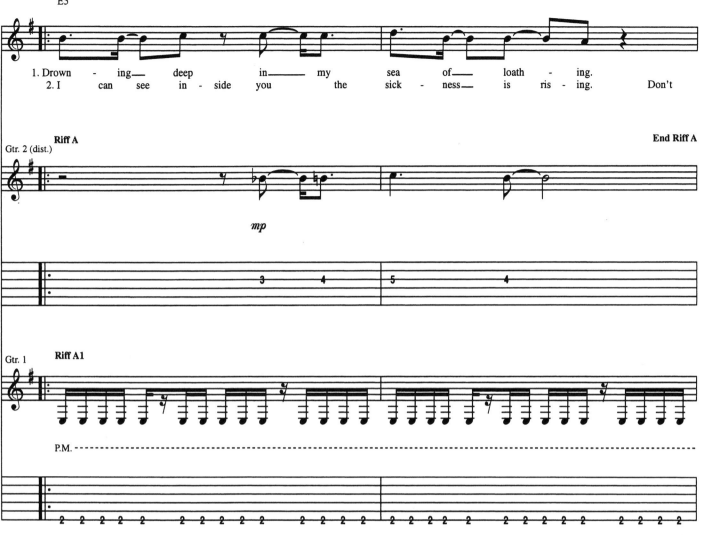

1. Drown - ing— deep in— my sea of— loath - ing.
2. I can see in - side you the sick - ness— is ris - ing. Don't

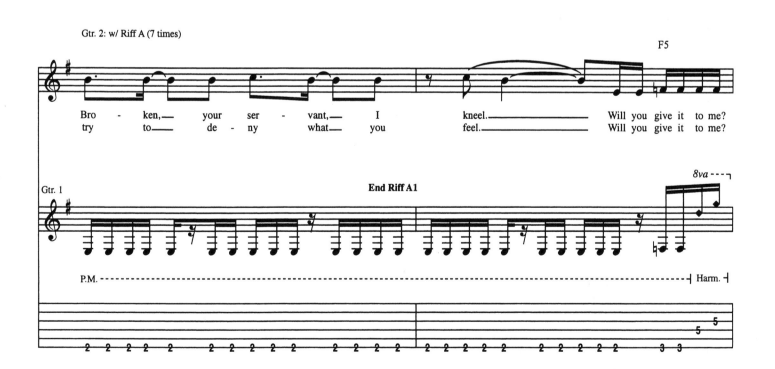

Bro - ken, your ser - vant, I kneel.———— Will you give it to me?
try to— de - ny what— you feel.———— Will you give it to me?

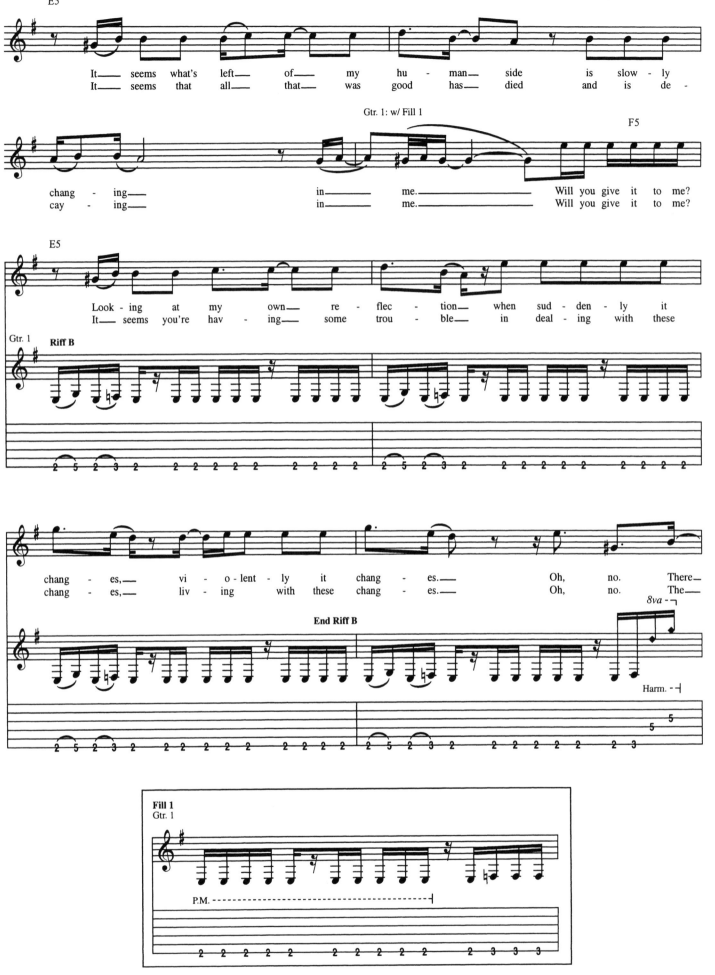

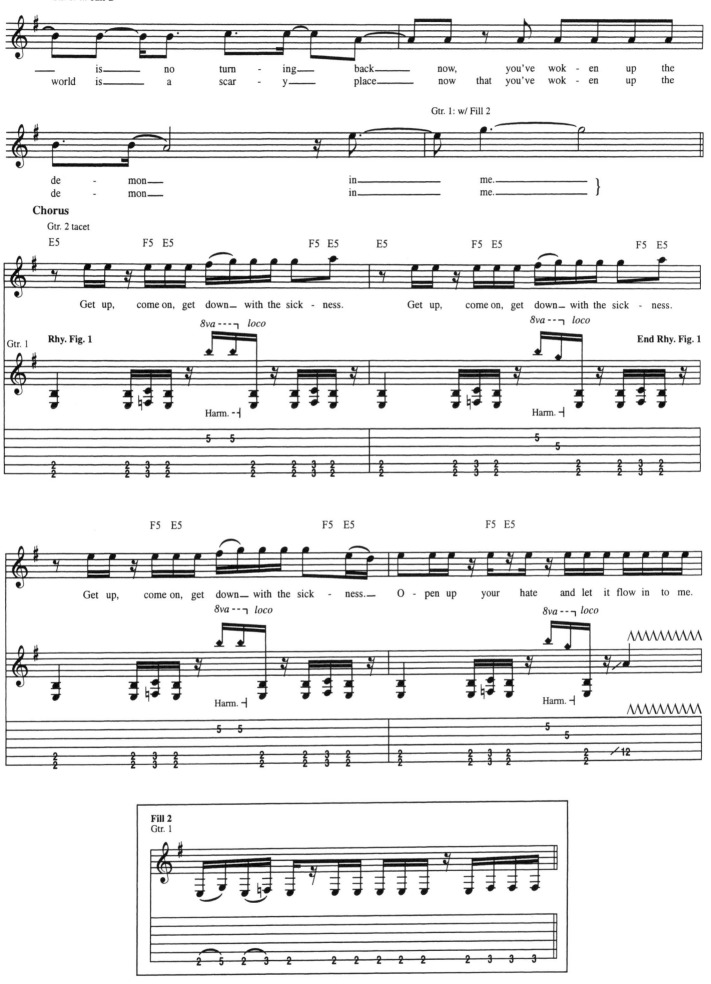

Gtr. 1: w/ Rhy. Fig. 1 (2 times)

Get up, come on, get down— with the sick - ness. You moth-er, get up, come on, get down— with the sick - ness. You

fuck - er, get up, come on, get down— with the sick - ness. Mad - ness is—— the gift that has been giv - en to me.

Gtr. 1: w/ Rhy. Fill 1

Mad - ness is—— the gift that has been giv - en to me.

Bridge

Play 3 times

And when I dream.

Gtr. 2   **Riff C**   **End Riff C**

Gtr. 1

Rhy. Fill 1
Gtr. 1

Outro-Chorus

Drain You

Words and Music by Kurt Cobain

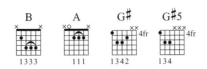

Tune down 1 step:
(low to high) D-G-C-F-A-D

Verse

Lively Rock ♩ = 136

1. One ba - by to ___ an - oth - er says ___ I'm luck - y ___ to have met ___

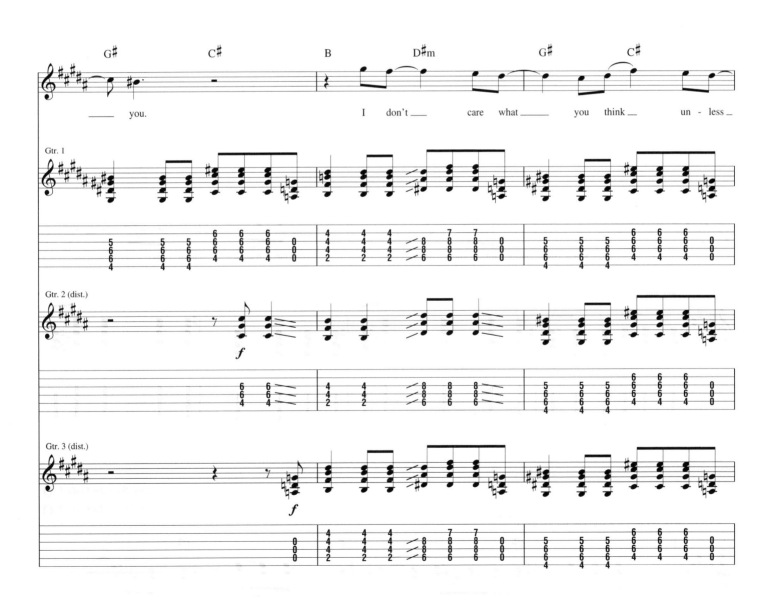

___ you.   I don't ___ care what ___ you think ___ un - less ___

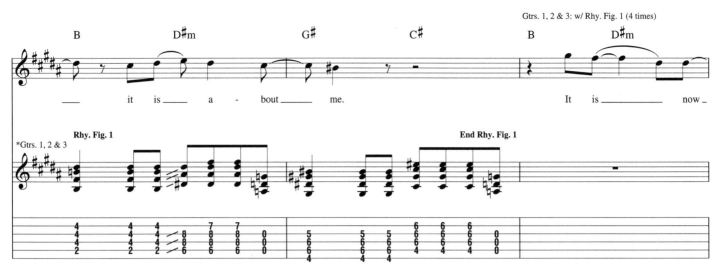

it is a-bout me. It is now

*Composite arrangement

my du-ty to com-plete-ly drain you. A trav-el through

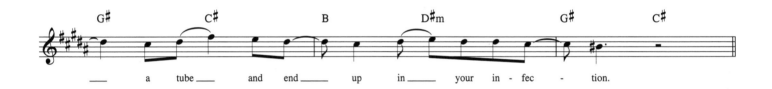

a tube and end up in your in-fec-tion.

𝄋 Chorus

Chew your meat for you, pass it back and forth.

In a pas-sion-ate kiss, from my mouth in yours

2nd time, To Coda 1 ⊕
3rd time, To Coda 2 ⊕

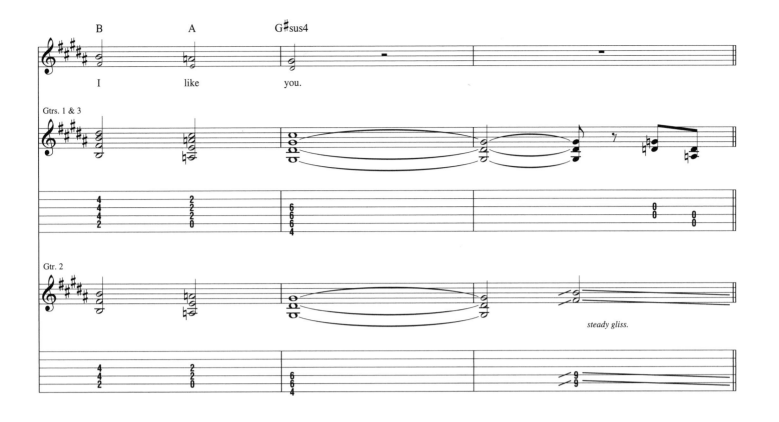

I like you.

Verse

2. With eyes so di - lat - ed I've be - come your pu - pil.

You've taught me ev - 'ry - thing with - out a poi - son ap - ple.

The wa - ter is so yel - low, I'm a health - y stu - dent.

D.S. al Coda 1

In - debt - ed and so grate - ful. Vac - uum out the flu - ids.

89

Interlude

Gtr. 2: w/ random fdbk. (next 15 meas.)
Gtr. 3: w/ random fdbk. (next 22 meas.)
Gtr. 5: w/ Rhy. Fig. 4 (24 times)

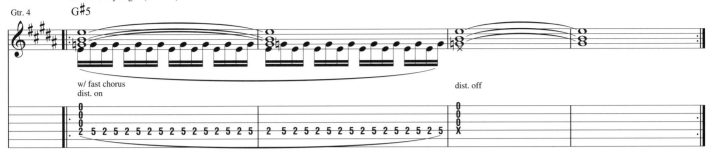

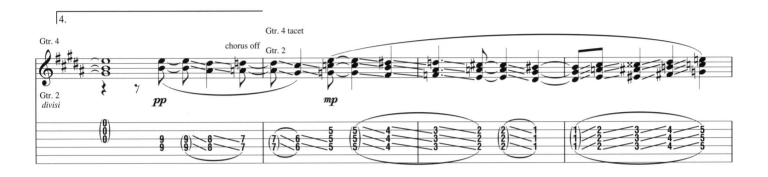

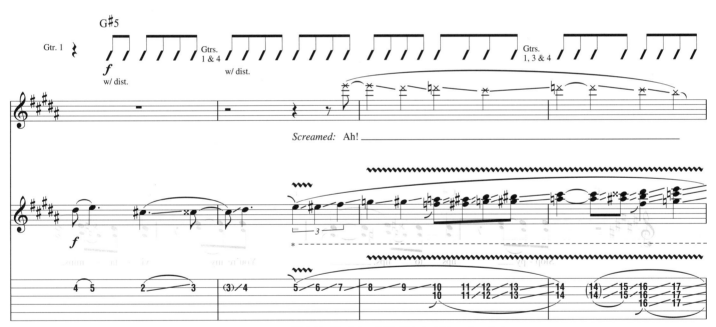

*Fret string(s) w/ edge of pick. Wriggle pick to produce vibrato.

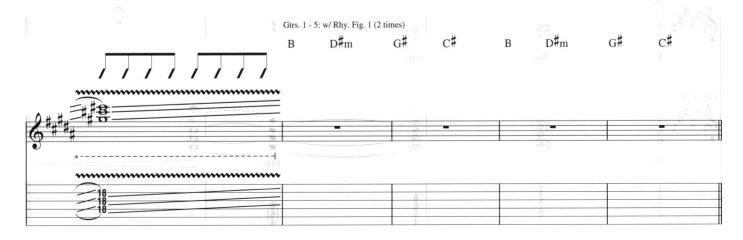

Verse

Gtrs. 1 - 5: w/ Rhy. Fig. 1 (8 times)

| B | D#m | G# | C# | B | D#m | G# | C# |

3. One ba - by to ___ an - oth - er says ___ I'm luck - y to have met you.

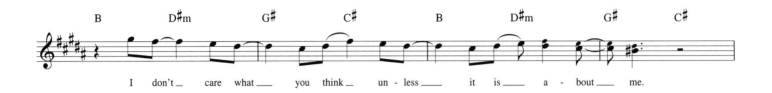

| B | D#m | G# | C# | B | D#m | G# | C# |

I don't ___ care what ___ you think ___ un - less ___ it is ___ a - bout ___ me.

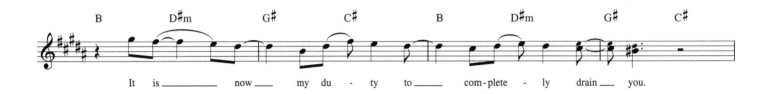

| B | D#m | G# | C# | B | D#m | G# | C# |

It is ___ now ___ my du - ty to ___ com - plete - ly drain ___ you.

D.S. al Coda 2

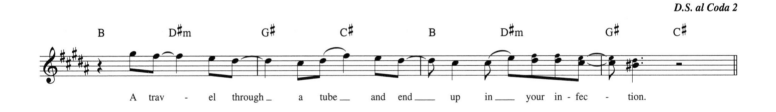

| B | D#m | G# | C# | B | D#m | G# | C# |

A trav - el through ___ a tube ___ and end ___ up in ___ your in - fec - tion.

⊕ Coda 2

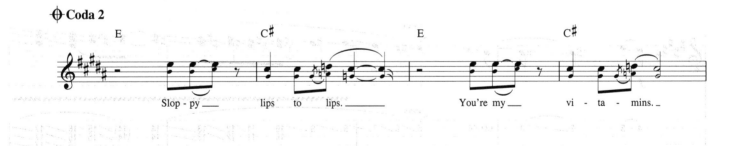

| E | C# | E | C# |

Slop - py ___ lips to lips. ___ You're my ___ vi - ta - mins. ___

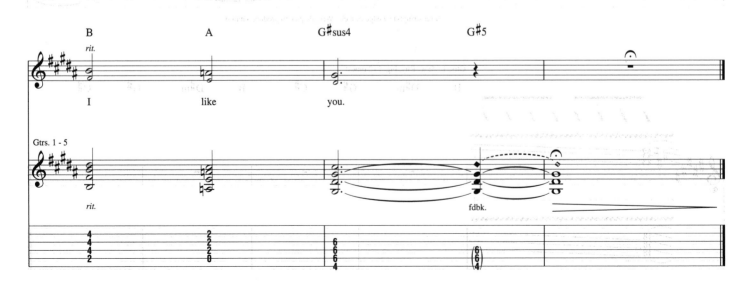

| B | A | G#sus4 | G#5 |

I like you.

Gtrs. 1 - 5

rit.

rit.

fdbk.

E-Pro

Words and Music by Beck, Mike Simpson, John King, Michael Diamond, Adam Horovitz and Adam Yauch

Chorus

Gtrs. 1 & 2: w/ Riff A (4 times)
Gtr. 3: w/ Rhy. Fig. 1 (4 times)

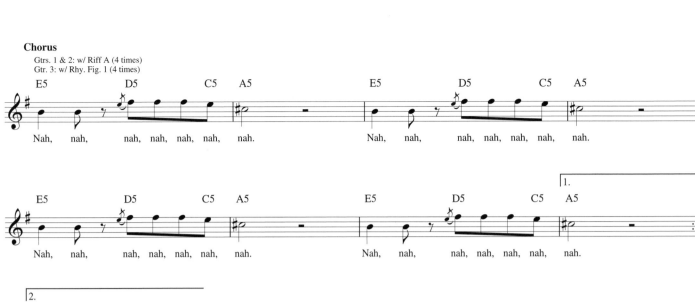

Nah, nah, nah, nah, nah, nah, nah. Nah, nah, nah, nah, nah, nah, nah.

1.

Nah, nah, nah, nah, nah, nah, nah. Nah, nah, nah, nah, nah, nah, nah.

2.

Bridge

nah. I won't give up that ghost. It's sick the way these tongues are twist-ed. The

Voc. Fig. 1   End Voc. Fig. 1

(Oo. ____   Oo. ____   Oo.) ____

Bkgd. Voc.: w/ Voc. Fig. 1 (3 times)

good in us ___ (is) all we know. There's too much left to taste _ that's bit-ter. I won't give up that ghost. _ It's

sick the way _ these tongues are twist-ed. The good in us ___ (is) all we know. _ There's too much left to taste _ that's bit-ter.

____   (Oo. _____   Oo.) ____

Chorus

Gtrs. 1 & 2: w/ Riff A (3 times)
Gtr. 3: w/ Rhy. Fig. 1 (2 times)

Nah, nah, nah, nah, nah, nah, nah. Nah, nah, nah, nah, nah, nah, nah.

Gtr. 3: w/ Rhy. Fig. 2

Nah, nah, nah, nah, nah, nah, nah. Nah, nah, nah, nah, nah, nah,

Gtr. 1: w/ Riff A (last meas.)
Gtrs. 1 & 2: w/ Riff A (4 times)
Gtr. 3: w/ Rhy. Fig. 1 (2 1/2 times)

A5 E5 D5 C5 A5

nah. Nah, nah, nah, nah, nah, nah, nah.

E5 D5 C5 A5 E5 D5 C5

*Voc. Fig. 2 End Voc. Fig. 2

Nah, nah, nah, nah, nah, nah, nah. Nah, nah, nah, nah, nah, nah,

(Nah, nah, yeah, yeah.)

*Applies to bkgd. voc. only.

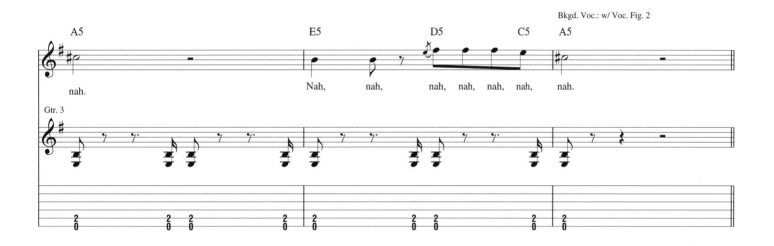

Bkgd. Voc.: w/ Voc. Fig. 2

A5 E5 D5 C5 A5

nah. Nah, nah, nah, nah, nah, nah, nah.

Gtr. 3

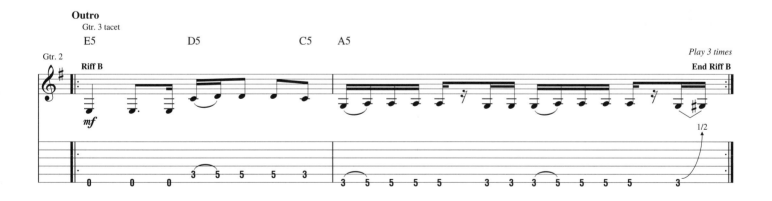

Outro
Gtr. 3 tacet

E5 D5 C5 A5

Gtr. 2

Riff B

Play 3 times

End Riff B

mf

1/2

3rd time, Begin fade *Fade out*

Gtr. 2: w/ Riff B Gtrs. 1 & 2: w/ Riff A (till fade) Segue to *"Qué Onda Guero"*
Gtr. 3: w/ Rhy. Fig. 1 (till fade)

E5 D5 C5 A5 E5 D5 C5 A5 *Play 4 times* A5

Nah, nah, nah, nah, nah, nah, nah.

Everlong

Words and Music by David Grohl

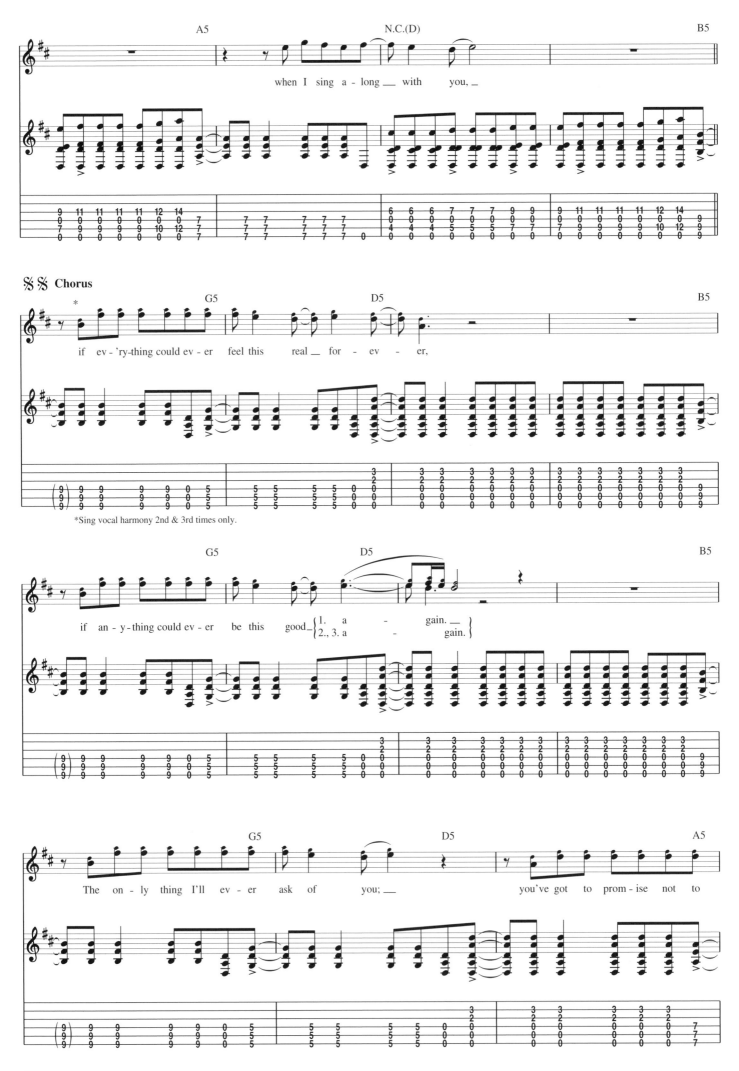

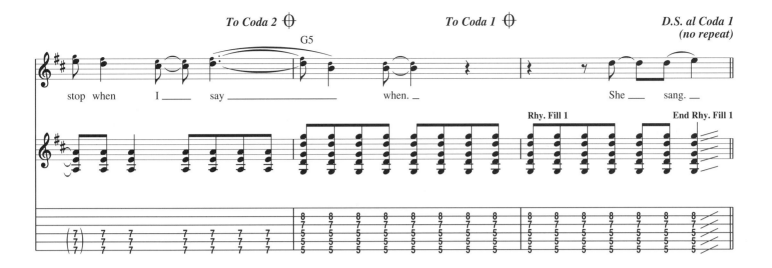

stop when I _____ say _____ when. _____ She _____ sang. _____

Rhy. Fill 1   End Rhy. Fill 1

⊕ *Coda 1*

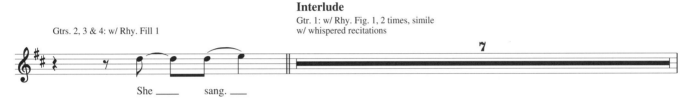

Gtrs. 2, 3 & 4: w/ Rhy. Fill 1

Interlude
Gtr. 1: w/ Rhy. Fig. 1, 2 times, simile
w/ whispered recitations

She _____ sang. _____

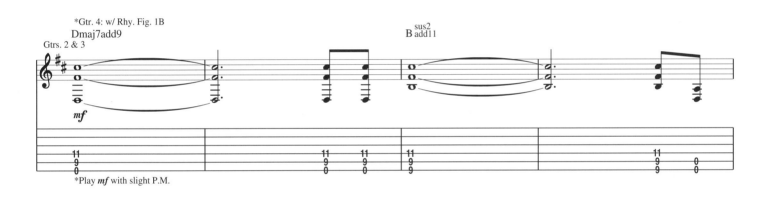

*Gtr. 4: w/ Rhy. Fig. 1B
Dmaj7add9
Gtrs. 2 & 3

B$\flat$add11 sus2

*Play *mf* with slight P.M.

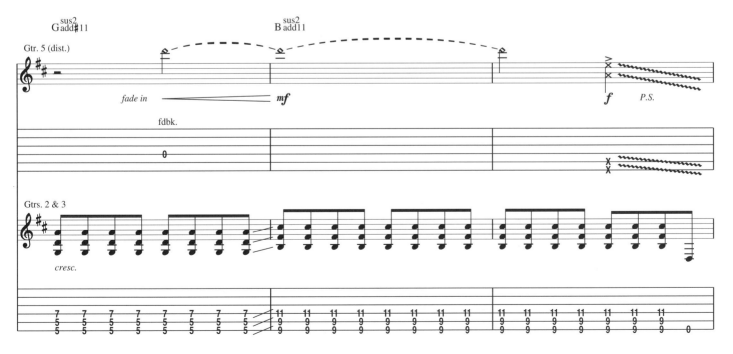

G$\sharp$add11 sus2
Gtr. 5 (dist.)

B$\flat$add11 sus2

fade in _____ *mf*

fdbk.

f   P.S.

Gtrs. 2 & 3

cresc.

99

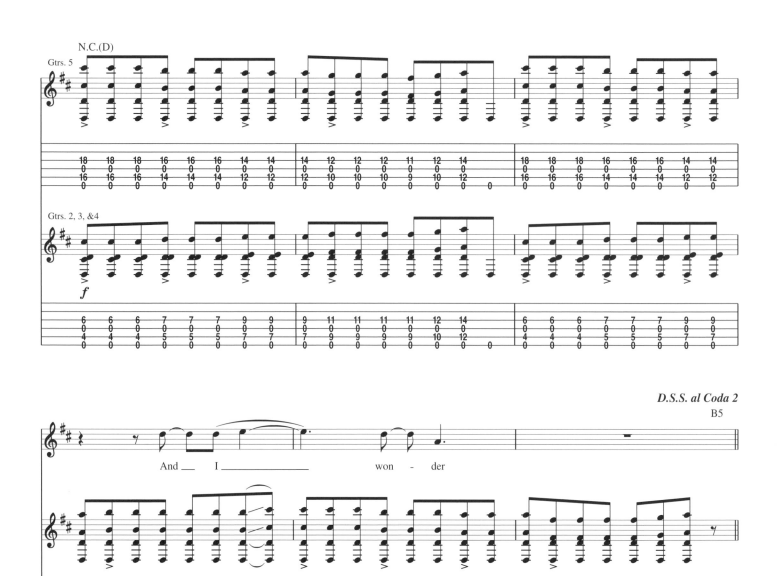

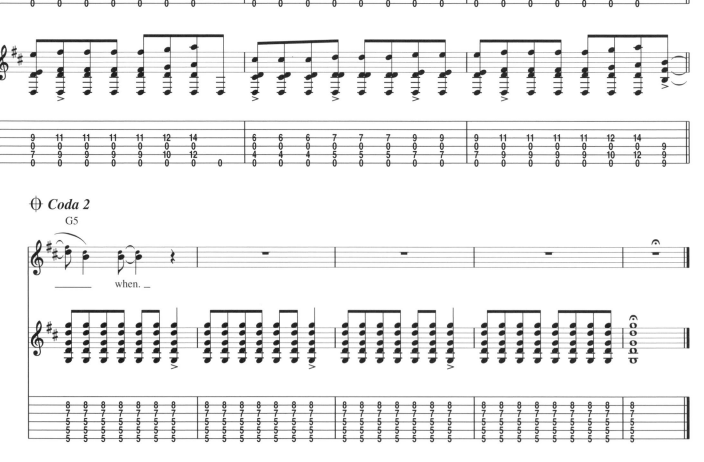

Eye of the Tiger

Theme from ROCKY III

Words and Music by Frank Sullivan and Jim Peterik

Verse

Gtr. 2 tacet   Gtr. 1: w/ Riff A, 2 times

1. Ris - in' up,   back on the street,   did my time,   took my chanc - es.

Went the dis - tance, now I'm back on _ my feet,   just a man   and his will to sur - vive. _

Verse

Gtr. 1: w/ Riff A, 2 times, 1st time
Gtr. 1 tacet, 2nd time

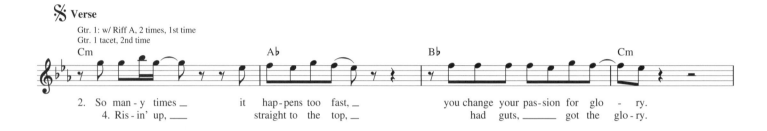

2. So man - y times _   it hap - pens too fast, _   you change your pas - sion for glo - ry.
4. Ris - in' up, ___   straight to the top, _   had guts, _____ got the glo - ry.

Gtr. 1: w/ Riff A, 2nd time

Don't lose your grip _   on the dreams of _ the past,   you must fight   just to keep   them a - live. _   It's the
Went the dis - tance, now I'm not gon - na stop,   just a man   and his will   to sur - vive. _

Chorus

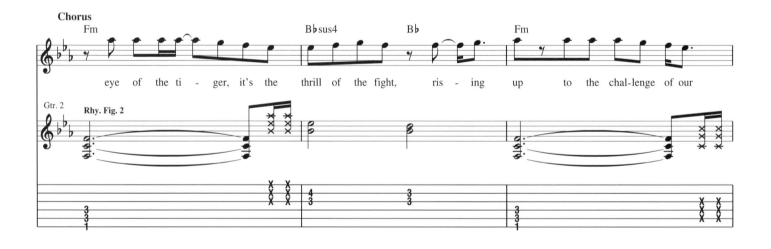

eye of the ti - ger, it's the   thrill of the fight,   ris - ing up   to the chal - lenge of our

Gtr. 2
Rhy. Fig. 2

ri - val.   And _ the   last known sur - vi - vor stalks his   prey in the night,   and _ he's

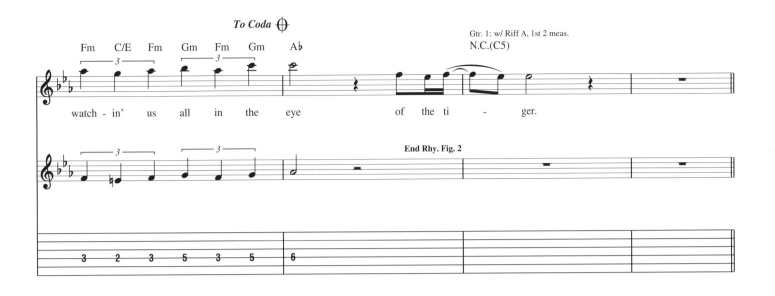

To Coda

Fm C/E Fm Gm Fm Gm Ab   Gtr. 1: w/ Riff A, 1st 2 meas.
                                                N.C.(C5)

watch-in' us all in the eye of the ti - ger.

End Rhy. Fig. 2

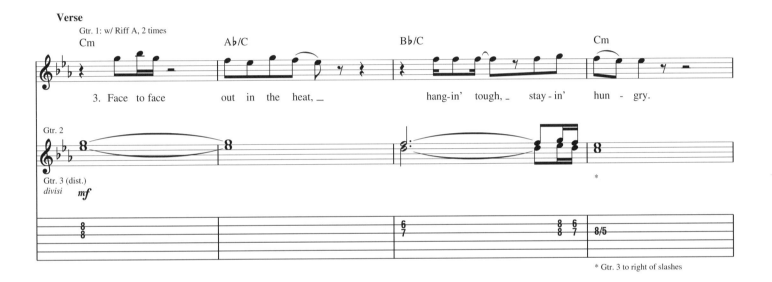

Verse

Gtr. 1: w/ Riff A, 2 times

Cm   Ab/C   Bb/C   Cm

3. Face to face out in the heat, __ hang-in' tough, __ stay-in' hun - gry.

Gtr. 2

Gtr. 3 (dist.)
divisi *mf*

* Gtr. 3 to right of slashes

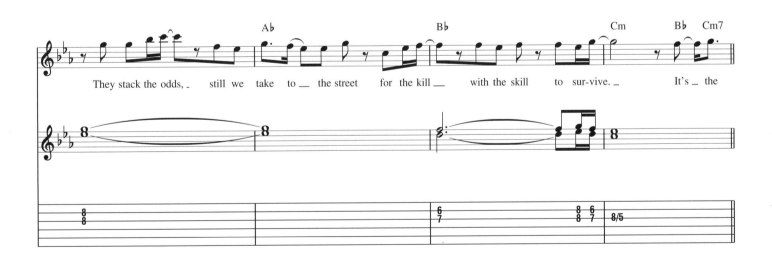

Ab   Bb   Cm   Bb Cm7

They stack the odds, __ still we take to __ the street for the kill __ with the skill to sur-vive. __ It's __ the

Chorus

Gtr. 2: w/ Rhy. Fig. 2
Gtrs. 1 & 3 tacet

Fm   Bbsus4 Bb   Fm

eye of the ti - ger, it's the thrill of the fight, ris - ing up to the chal - lenge of our

103

ri - val. And __ the last known sur - vi - vor stalks his prey in the night, and __ he's

Gtr. 1: w/ Riff A
N.C.(C5)

D.S. al Coda

watch- in' us all in the eye of the ti - ger.

Coda

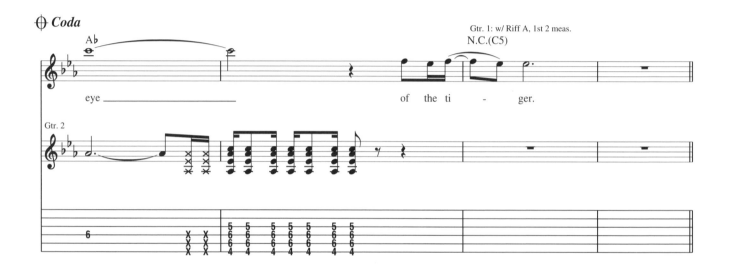

Gtr. 1: w/ Riff A, 1st 2 meas.
N.C.(C5)

eye _____ of the ti - ger.

Gtr. 2

Outro

Gtr. 1: w/ Riff A, till fade
Gtr. 2: w/ Rhy. Fig. 1, 2 times

The eye of the ti - ger.

Gtr. 2: w/ Rhy. Fig. 1A, till fade

The eye of the ti - ger. _____

Begin Fade

The eye of the ti - ger. _____

Fade Out

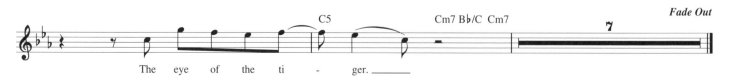

The eye of the ti - ger. _____

Feel the Pain

Words and Music by Joseph Mascis Jr.

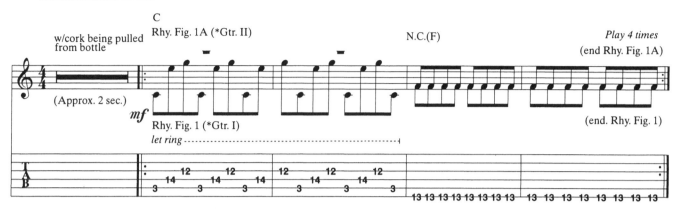

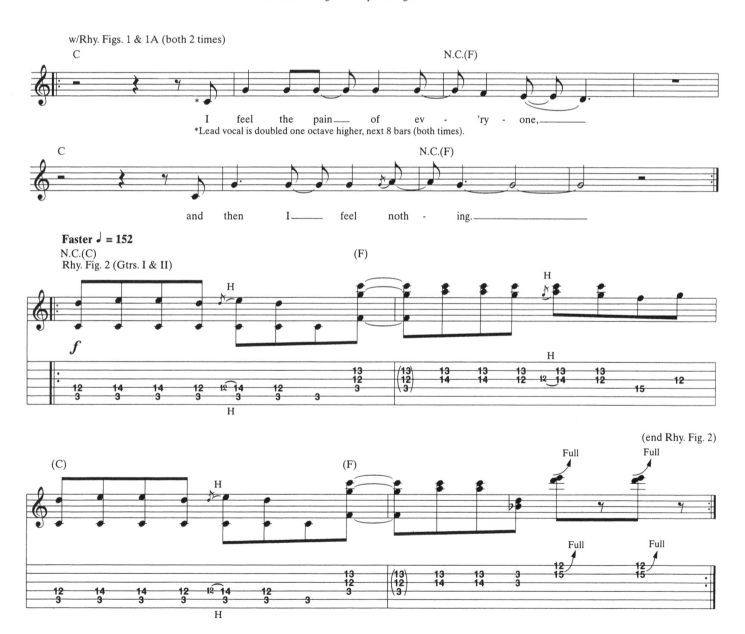

*Gtrs. I & II w/capo at 3rd fret. TAB numbers
indicate actual frets, relative to nut.
All 3's are thought of as open strings.

I feel the pain of ev - 'ry - one,
*Lead vocal is doubled one octave higher, next 8 bars (both times).

and then I feel noth - ing.

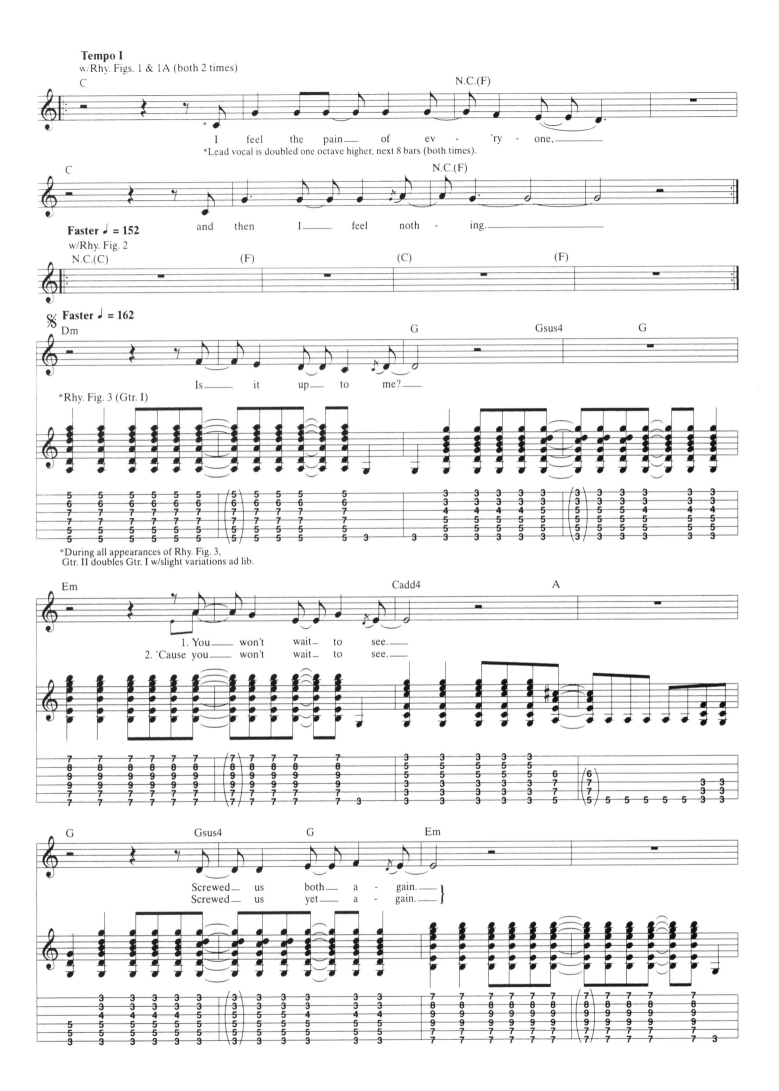

Float On

Words and Music by Isaac Brock, Eric Judy and Dann Gallucci

*Chord symbols reflect overall harmony.

he just drove off, some-times life's O. K. _____ I ran my mouth off a bit too much, oh, what did I say?

Well, you just laughed it off, _____ it was all O. K.

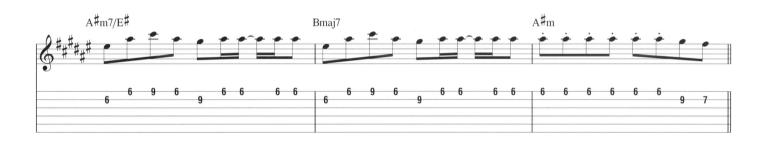

𝄋 **Chorus**

1st time, Gtr. 2 tacet
2nd time, Gtr. 2: w/ Fill 1

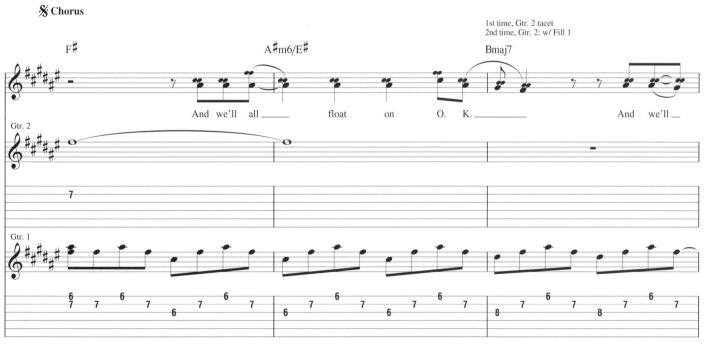

And we'll all _____ float on O. K. _____ And we'll _____

Fill 1
Gtr. 2

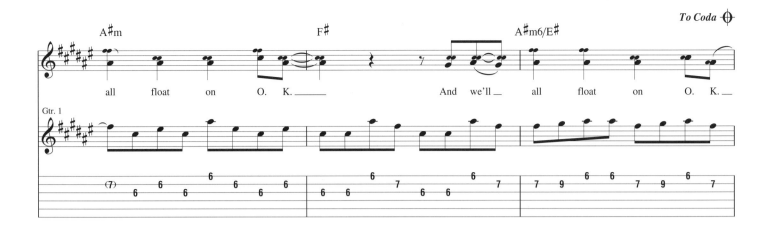

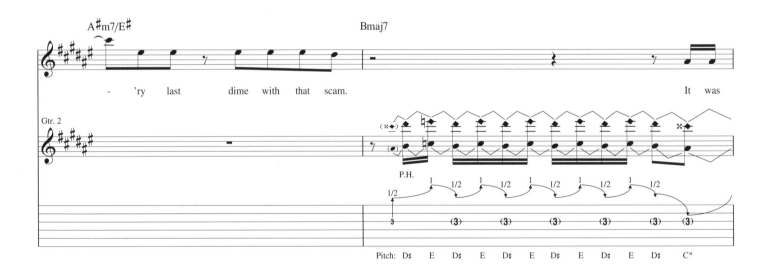

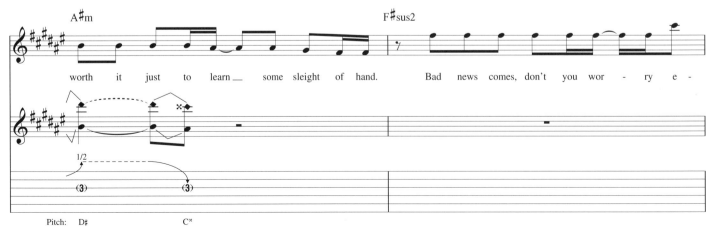

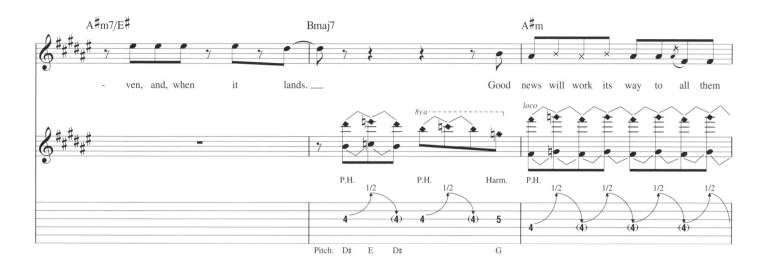

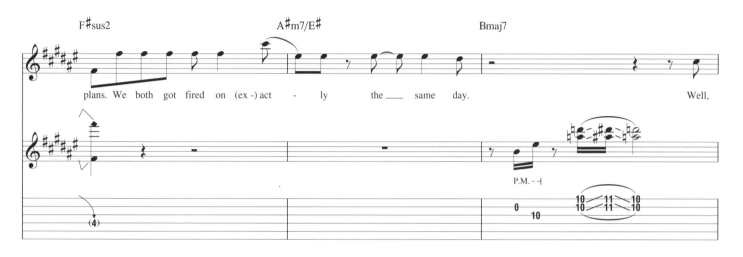

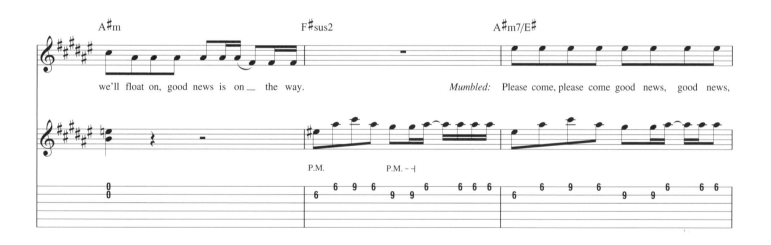

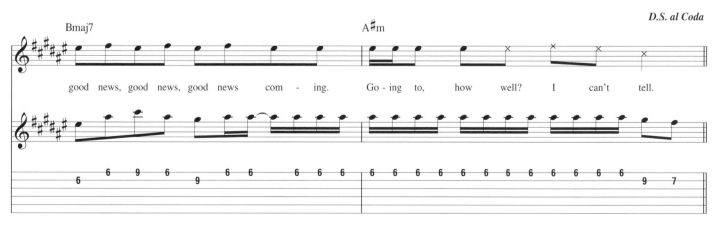

Coda

Bridge

Gtr. 1: w/ Rhy. Fig. 1 (2 times)

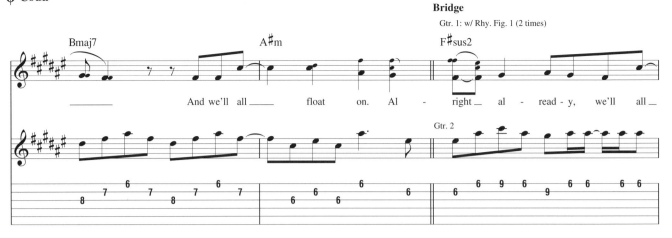

And we'll all ___ float on. Al - right ___ al - read - y, we'll all ___

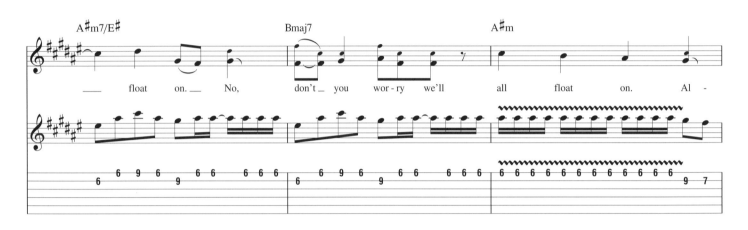

___ float on. ___ No, don't ___ you wor - ry we'll all float on. Al -

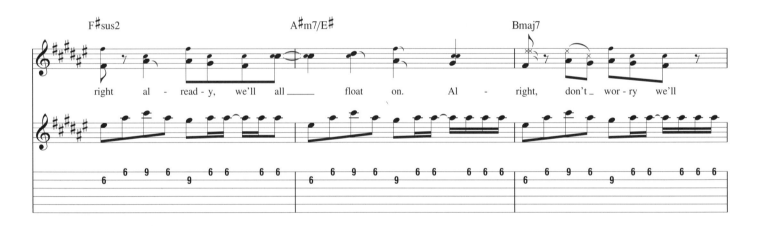

right al - read - y, we'll all ___ float on. Al - right, don't ___ wor - ry we'll

Interlude

Gtrs. 1 & 2 tacet

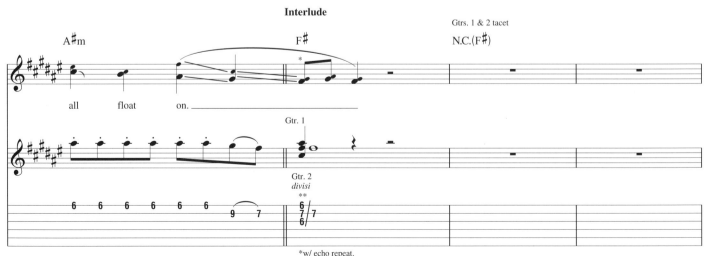

all float on. _____

*w/ echo repeat.

**Gtr. 1 to left of slash in tab.

Gtrs. 3 & 4 tacet

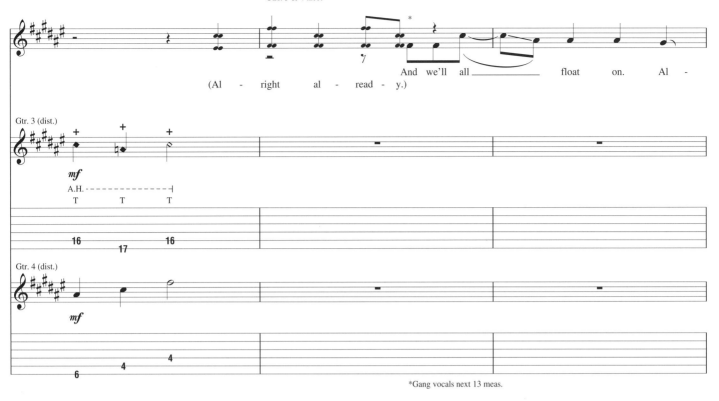

And we'll all _____ float on. Al -
(Al - right al - read - y.)

Gtr. 3 (dist.)

mf

A.H.

*Gang vocals next 13 meas.

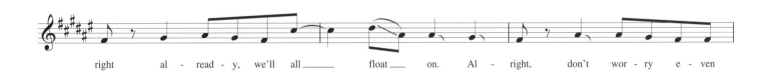

right al - read - y, we'll all _____ float ___ on. Al - right, don't wor - ry e - ven

if things end up a bit too heav - y. We'll all _____ float ___ on. Al -

w/ Voc. ad lib. (next 8 meas.)
Gtr. 1: w/ Rhy. Fig. 1 (2 times)

F#sus2   A#m7/E#   Bmaj7

right al - read - y, we'll all _____ float on. Al - right al - read - y, we'll all _____

Gtr. 2

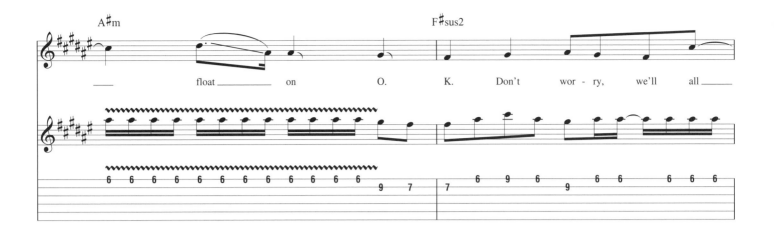

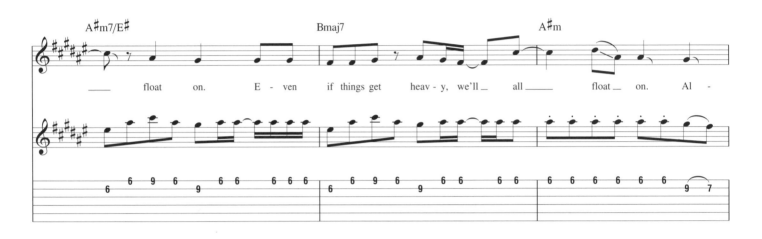

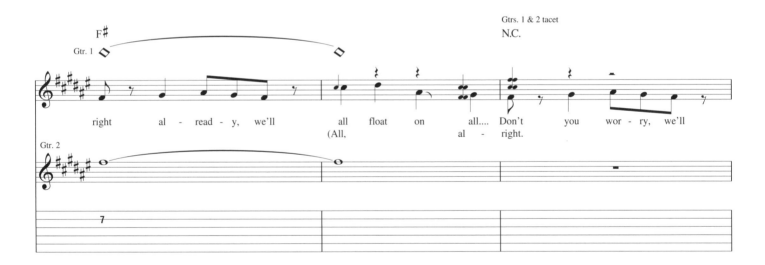

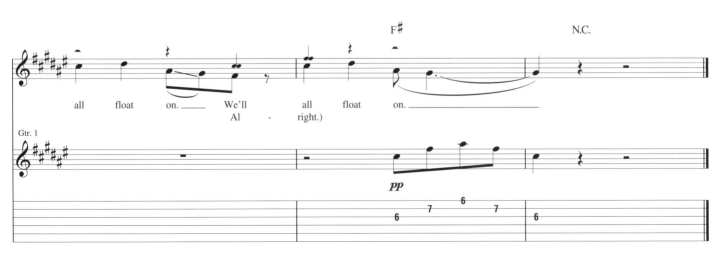

Give It Away

Words and Music by Anthony Kiedis, Flea, John Frusciante and Chad Smith

Gtr. 1: w/ Riff A, 1 1/2 times, simile

What I've got, you've got to get it, put it in you. What I've got, you've got to get it, put it in you.
Low brow, but I rock a lit-tle know how. No time for the pig-gies or the hoose-gow.

What I've got, you've got to get it, put it in you. Reel-ing with the feel-ing, don't stop, con-tin-ue.
Get smart, get down with the pow-er, nev-er been a bet-ter time than right now.

Re-a-lize __ I don't wan-na be a mi-ser, con-fide with Sly, you'll be the wi-ser.
Bob Mar-ley, po-et and a proph-et, Bob Mar-ley taught me how to off it.

To Coda 1
To Coda 2

Young blood is the lov-in' up-ri-ser. How come ev-'ry-bod-y wan-na keep it like the Kai-ser?
Bob Mar-ley walk-in' like he talk it. Good-ness me, can't you see I'm gon-na cough it?

Gtr. 1

Chorus
N.C.(A5)

Give it a-way, give it a-way, give it a-way now. __ Give it a-way, give it a-way, give it a-way now.

Two gtrs. arr. for one.

1.

Give it a-way, give it a-way, give it a-way now. __ I can't tell if I'm a king-pin or a pau-per!

Coda 2

Out-Chorus

Give it a-way, give it a-way, give it a-way now. _ Give it a-way, give it a-way, give it a-way, now. _

Give it a-way, give it a-way, give it a-way now. _ Give it a-way, give it a-way, give it a-way, now. _

Give it a-way now. Give it a-way now.

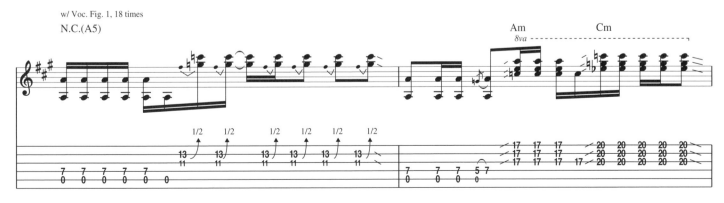

w/ Voc. Fig. 1, 18 times

Additional Lyrics

3. Lucky me, swimmin' in my ability,
Dancin' down on life with agility.
Come and drink it up from my fertility,
Blessed with a bucket of lucky mobility.

My mom, I love her 'cause she love me,
Long gone are the times when she scrub me.
Feelin' good, my brother gonna hug me,
Drink up my juice, young love, chug-a-lug me.

There's a river born to be a giver,
Keep you warm, won't let you shiver.
His heart is never gonna wither,
Come on everybody, time to deliver.

Go Your Own Way

Words and Music by Lindsey Buckingham

that I feel. If I could maybe I'd give

you my world. How can I

when you won't take __ it from __ me. _____

Chorus
w/Fill 1 (3rd time only)

You can go __ your __ own __ way. _____
Go __ your __ own __ way. _____

Fill 1

You can go your own way.

You can call it an - oth -

er lone - ly day.

You can go

your own way.

I Was Wrong

Words and Music by Michael Ness

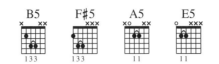

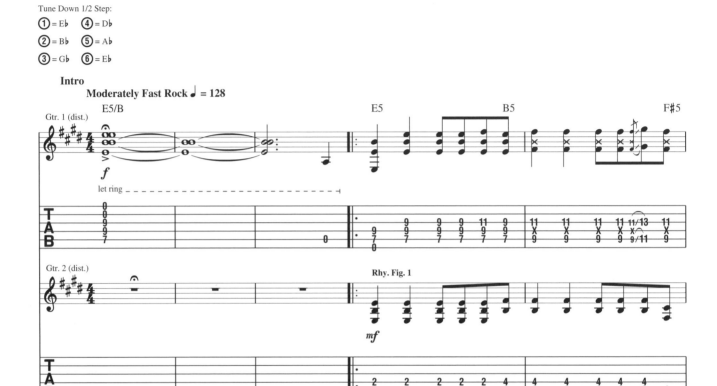

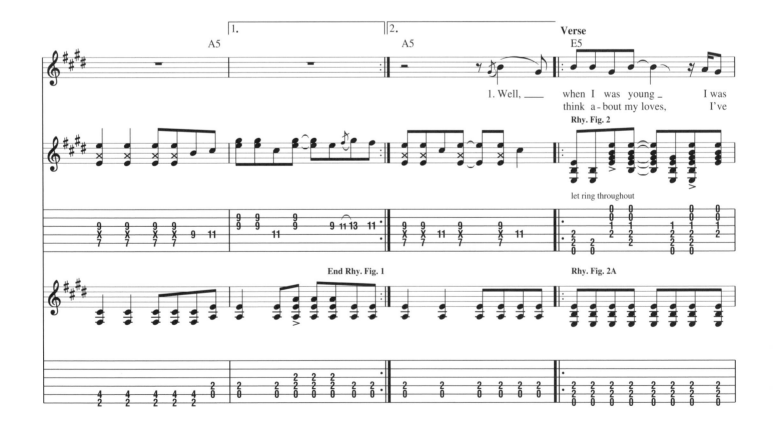

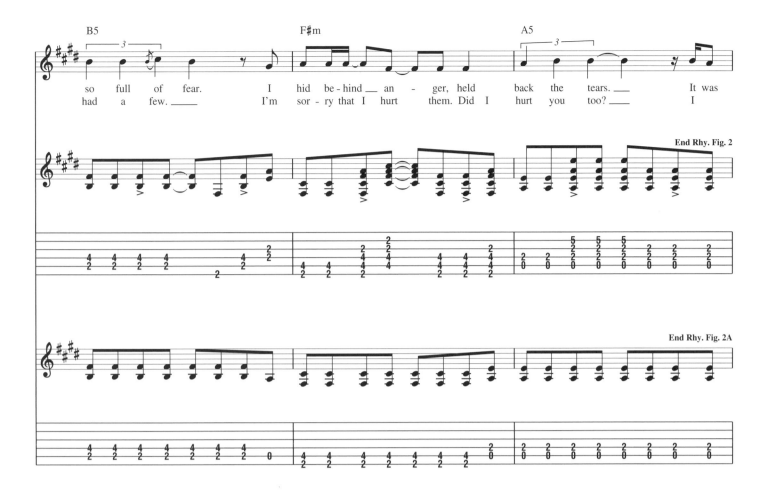

so full of fear.   I hid be-hind ___ an- ger, held back the tears. ___ It was
had a few. ___   I'm sor-ry that I hurt them. Did I hurt you too? ___   I

End Rhy. Fig. 2

End Rhy. Fig. 2A

Gtrs. 1 & 2: w/ Rhy. Figs. 2 & 2A, 3 times, simile

E5   B5   F#m

me a-gainst the world. ___   I was sure that I'd ___ win but the world fought back, ___ pun-ished me
took what I want-ed,   put my heart on the shelf.   How can you love when you

A5   E5   B5

for my sins. ___   I felt so a- lone, ___   so in- se- cure. ___   I
don't love your-self?   It was me 'gainst the world.   I was sure that I'd ___ win but the

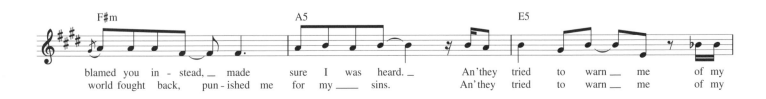

F#m   A5   E5

blamed you in-stead, ___ made sure I was heard.   An' they tried to warn ___ me of my
world fought back, pun-ished me for my ___ sins.   An' they tried to warn ___ me of my

e - vil ___ ways ___ but I could - n't hear ___ what they had to say. ___ I was
e - vil ___ ways ___ but I could - n't hear ___ what they had to say. ___ I was

𝄋 Chorus

Gtrs. 1 & 2: w/ Rhy. Figs. 2 & 2A, 2 times, simile

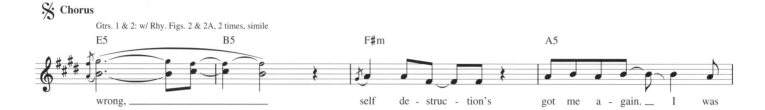

wrong, ___ self de - struc - tion's got me a - gain. ___ I was

To Coda ⊕

wrong, ___ I re - al - ized ___ now that I was wrong. ___ 2. An' I

Gtrs. 1 & 2: w/ Rhy. Figs. 2 & 2A, 2 times, simile

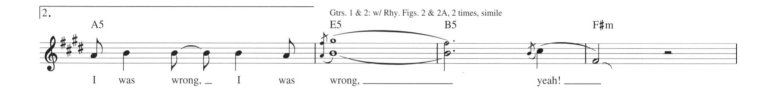

2.

I was wrong, ___ I was wrong, ___ yeah! ___

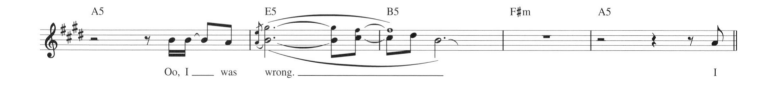

Oo, I ___ was wrong. ___ I

Bridge

grew up fast, ___ I grew up hard. ___ Some-thing was wrong ___ from the ve - ry start. ___ I was

let ring throughout

Gtrs. 1 & 2: w/ Rhy. Figs. 3 & 3A, 3 times, simile

fight - in' ev - 'ry-bod-y, __ I was __ fight - in' ev-'ry-thing. But the on - ly one __ that I

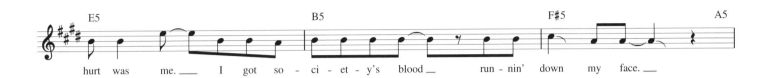

hurt was me. __ I got so - ci - et - y's blood __ run - nin' down my face. __

Some - bod - y help __ me get out - ta this place. __ How could some - one's __ bad

luck last so __ long? Un - til I ____ re - al - ized that I was so __ wrong. __

Guitar Solo

Gtr. 2: w/ Rhy. Fig. 1, 2 times, simile

Gtr. 1

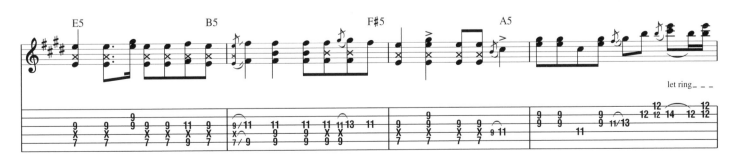

let ring

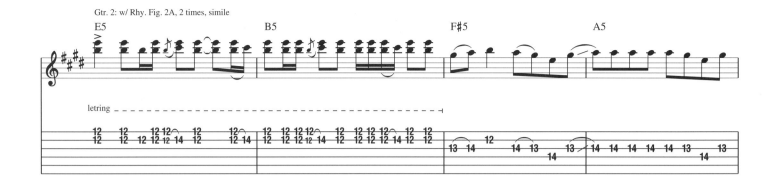

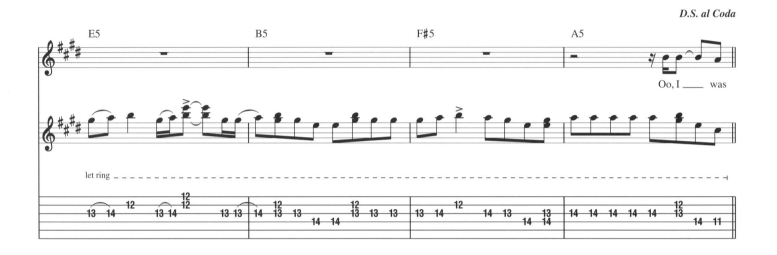

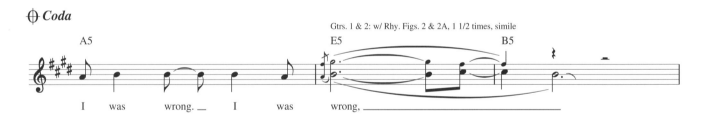

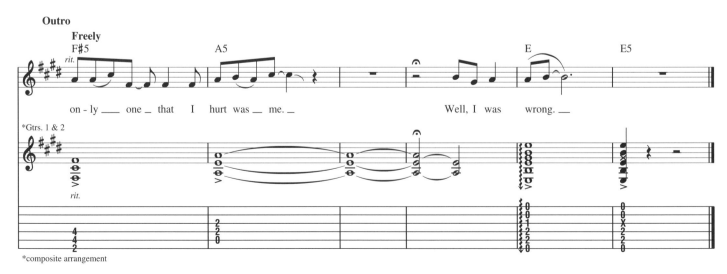

Let There Be Rock

Words and Music by Ronald Scott, Angus Young and Malcolm Young

gon - na do,_ But Tchai-kov-sky had_ the news._ He said "Let there be sound,"_

And there was sound.   "Let there be light,"_

And there was light.   "Let there be drums,"_

'N' there was drums.   "Let there be gui-

tar,"   There was gui-tar.   Let there be rock._

A5   *(vocal tacet on repeat)*

Rhythm figure 2   end Rhythm figure 2

Guitar solo

with Rhythm figure 2 (3 times)

B5

(with simile rhythm)

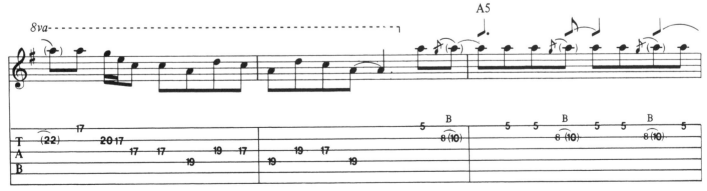

*play on repeats only.

And it came to pass, That Rock 'n' Roll was born. All a-

cross the land every rockin' band, Was blowin' up a storm. And the

guitar man got famous, The businessman got rich. And in

ev'ry bar there was a superstar, With a seven year itch.

There were fifty million fingers,

Learnin' how to play. And you could hear the fingers pickin',

And this is what they__ had to say.__ Let there be light,__

__ sound,

drums, gui - tar, Ow!__ "Let there be rock."

A5

(vocal tacet, guitar 2 enters on repeat)

with Rhythm figure 2 (2 times)

guitar 2

with Rhythm figure 2 (3 times)

B5

(with simile rhythm)

A5

G5

with feedback

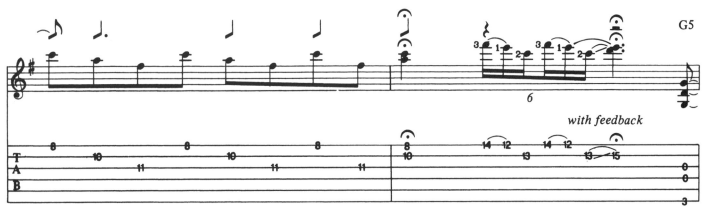

a tempo
with Rhythm figure 1 (4 times)

play 4 times
(vocal enters on
fourth time through)

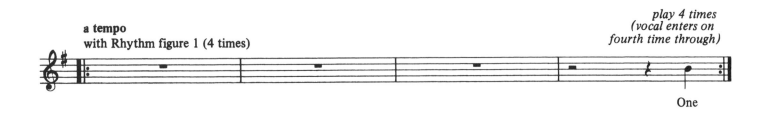

One

Livin' on a Prayer

Words and Music by Jon Bon Jovi, Desmond Child and Richie Sambora

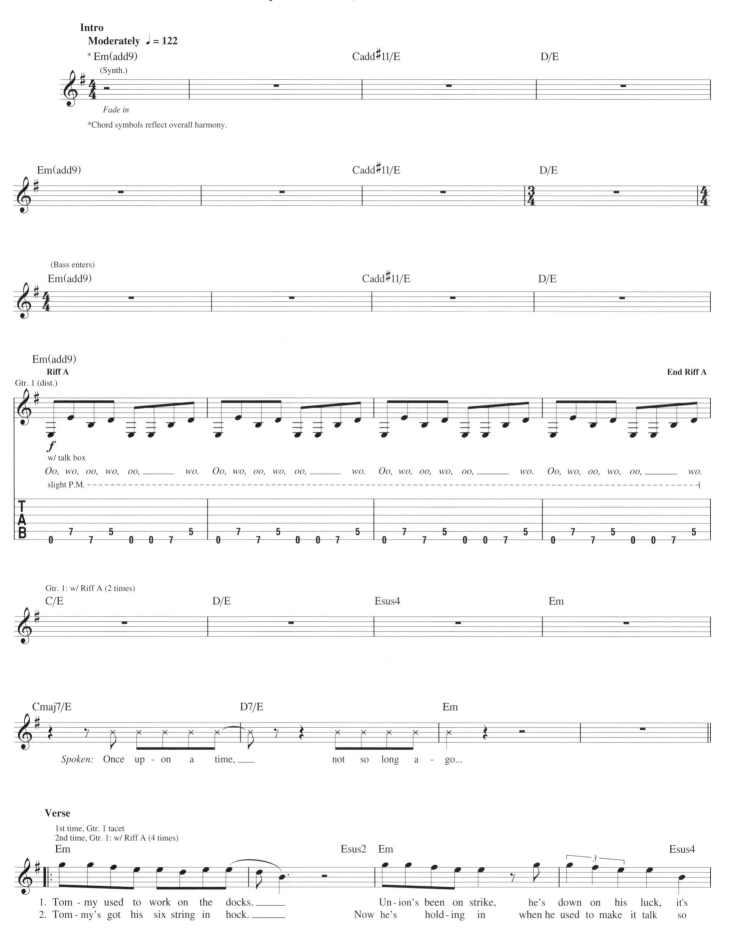

146

Lump

Words and Music by Chris Ballew, Dave Dederer and Jason Finn

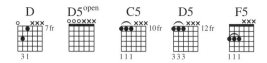

Drop D tuning; down 1/2 step:
(low to high) Db-Ab-Db-Gb-Bb-Eb

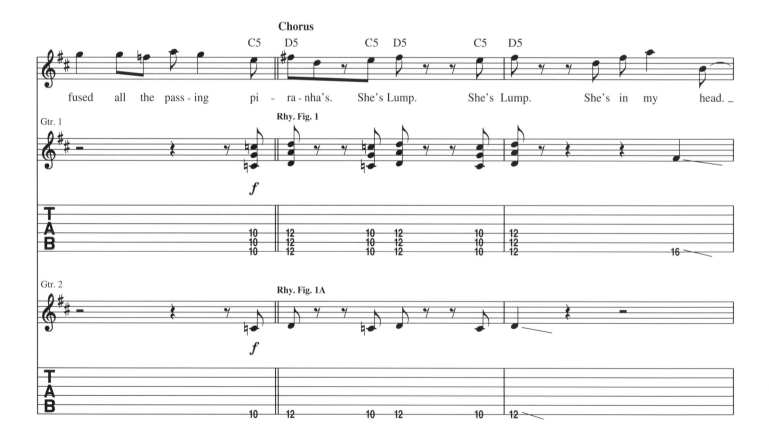

She's Lump. She's Lump. She's

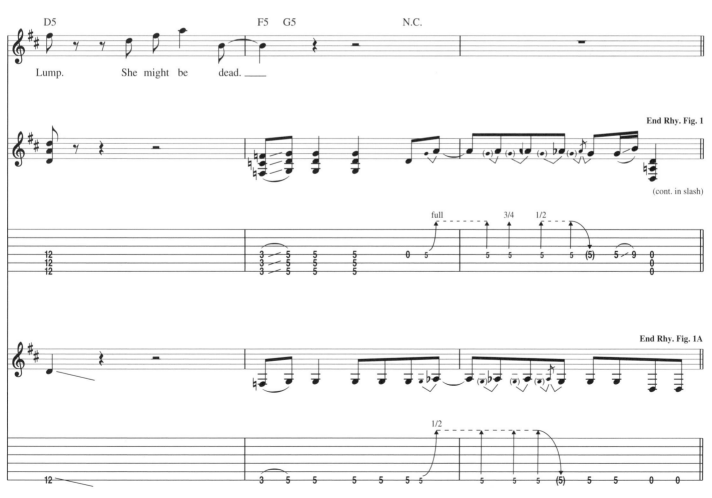

Lump. She might be dead. ____

End Rhy. Fig. 1

(cont. in slash)

End Rhy. Fig. 1A

152

Outro

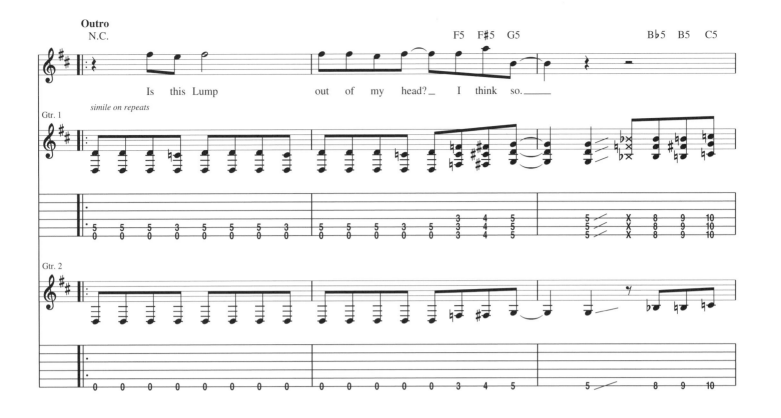

Is this Lump out of my head?__ I think so._____

simile on repeats

Gtr. 1

Gtr. 2

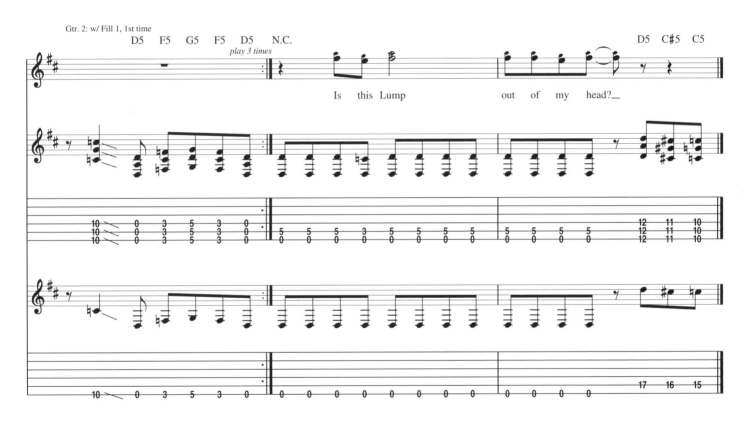

Gtr. 2: w/ Fill 1, 1st time

play 3 times

Is this Lump out of my head?__

Fill 1

Gtr. 2

Man in the Box

Written by Jerry Cantrell, Layne Staley, Sean Kinney and Michael Starr

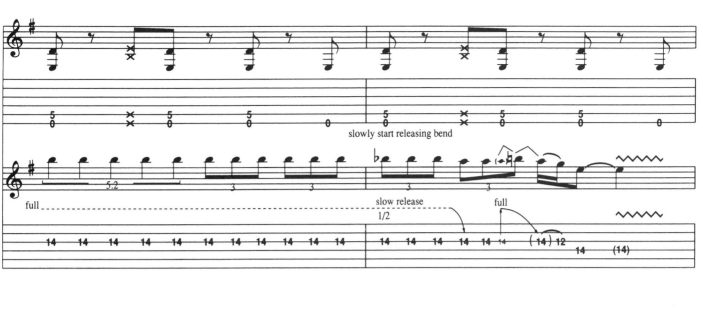

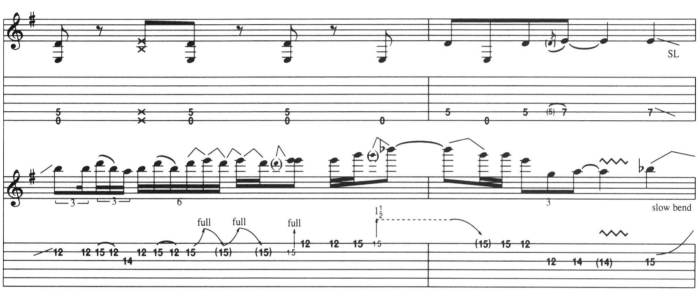

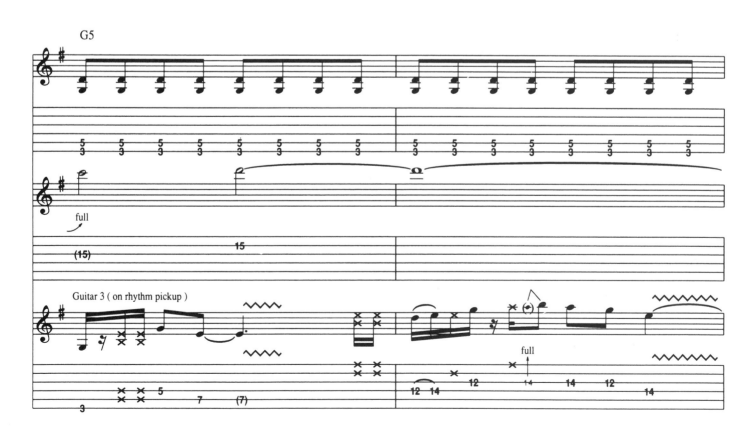

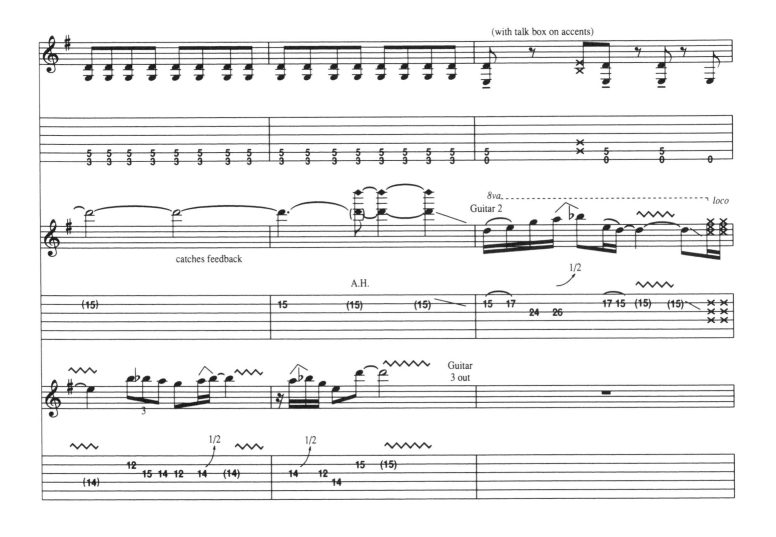

Coda

(Guitar 1 continues rhythm fig. 1 two more times)
Guitar 2 (Guitar with wah-wah)

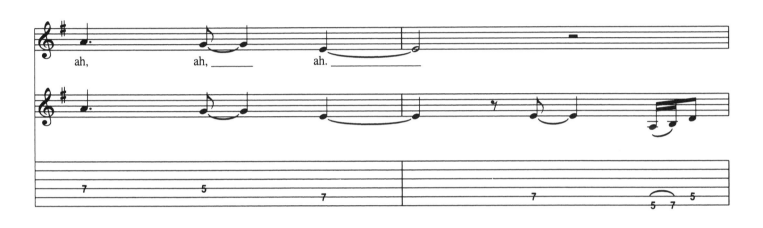

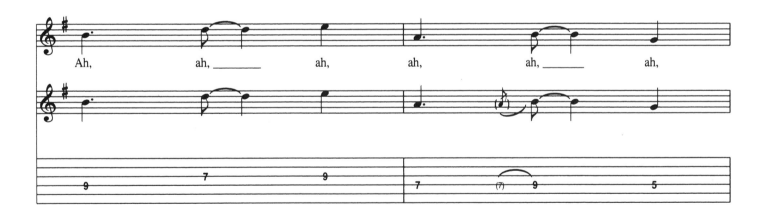

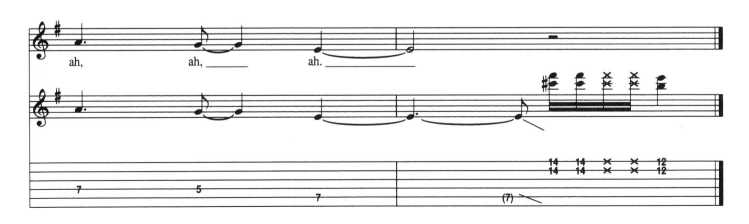

Mountain Song

Words and Music by Jane's Addiction

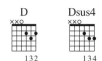

Verse

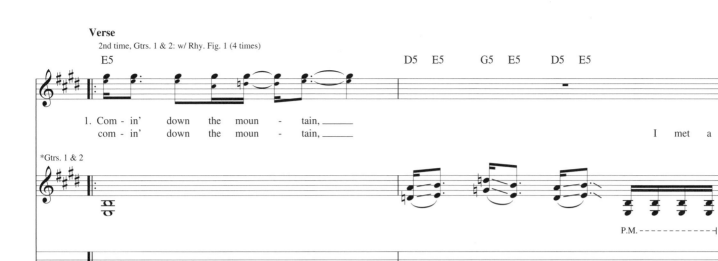

1. Com - in' down the moun - tain, _____ com - in' down the moun - tain, _____ I met a

*Gtrs. 1 & 2

P.M. - - - - - - - - - - - |

*Composite arrangement

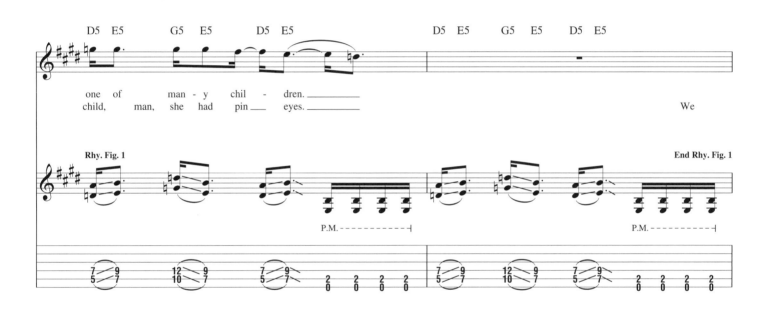

one of man - y chil - dren. _____
child, man, she had pin _____ eyes. _____ We

Rhy. Fig. 1 **End Rhy. Fig. 1**

P.M. - - - - - - - - - - - | P.M. - - - - - - - - - - |

Gtrs. 1 & 2: w/ Rhy. Fig. 1 (2 times)

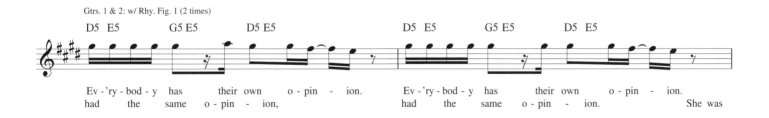

Ev-'ry-bod-y has their own o-pin - ion. Ev-'ry-bod-y has their own o-pin - ion.
had the same o-pin - ion, had the same o-pin - ion. She was

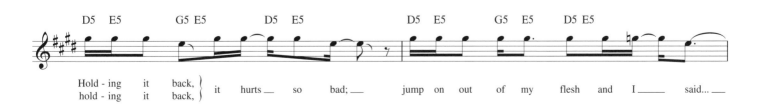

Hold - ing it back, } it hurts _____ so bad; _____ jump on out of my flesh and I _____ said... _____
hold - ing it back, }

Chorus

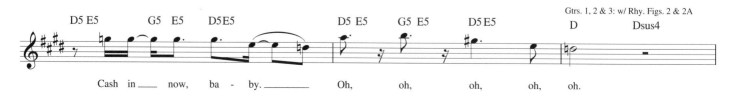

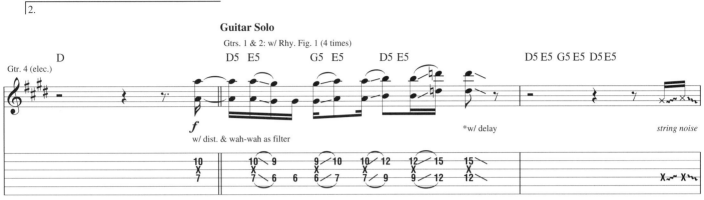

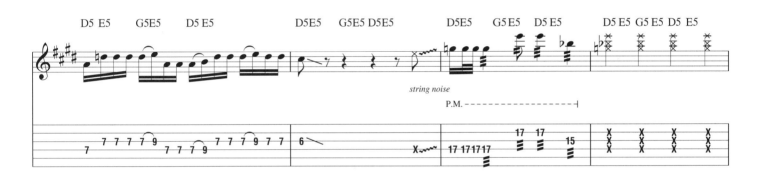

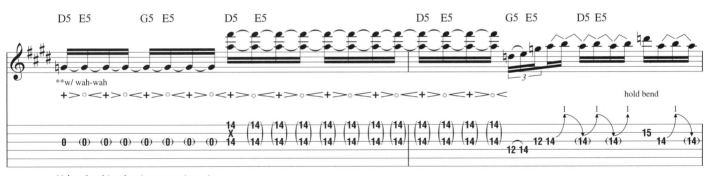

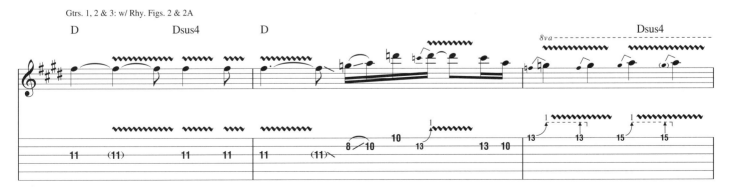

Outro

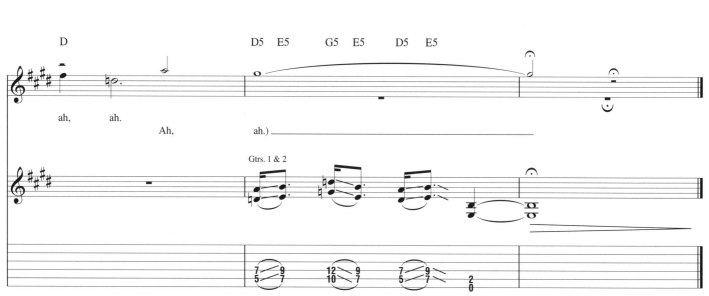

My Own Worst Enemy

Words and Music by Jeremy Popoff, Jay Popoff, Kevin Baldes and Allen Shellenberger

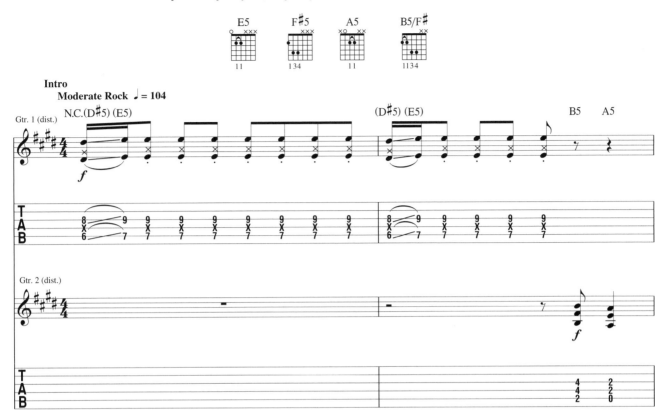

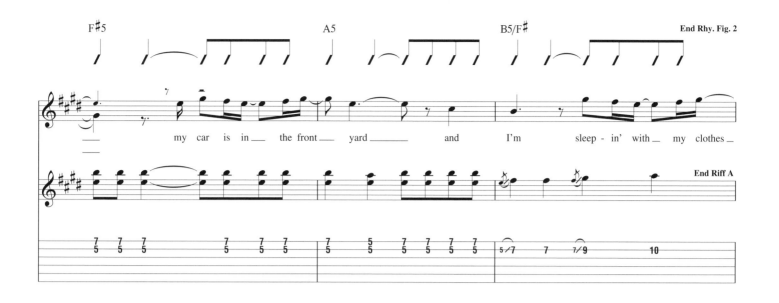

my car is in___ the front___ yard_____ and I'm sleep-in' with___ my clothes___

Gtr. 1: w/ Riff A, 1st & 2nd times; tacet 3rd time
Gtr. 2: w/ Rhy. Fig. 2

To Coda ⊕

___ on.___   I came in through___ the win - dow_____ last night___ and you're___

1.
Gtrs. 1 & 2: w/ Rhy. Figs. 1 & 1A

___ gone,   gone.___

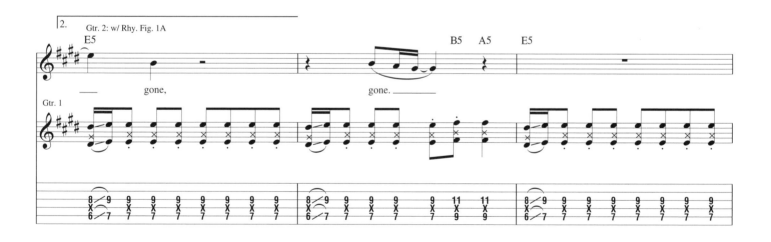

2.
Gtr. 2: w/ Rhy. Fig. 1A

___ gone,   gone.___

Guitar Solo
Gtr. 2: w/ Rhy. Fig. 1A

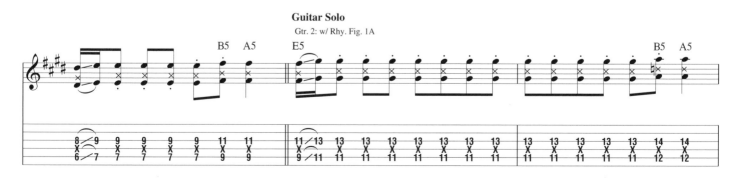

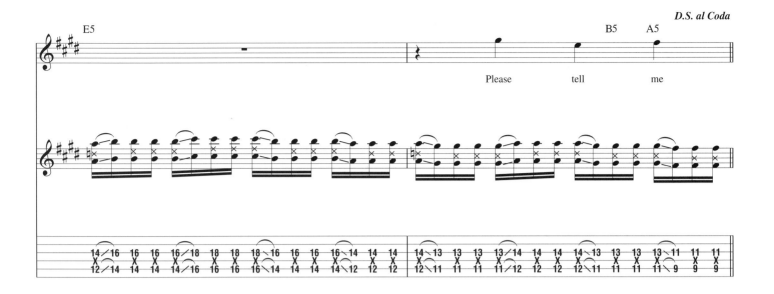

E5   B5   A5

Please tell me

Coda

Gtr. 1: w/ Riff A, 2 times
Gtr. 2: w/ Rhy. Fig. 2, 2 times

B5/F♯   E5   F♯5

night. _____ It's no sur - prise __ to me, I am __ my own __ worst en - e - my. __
(Ah, hoo. _____ Ah,

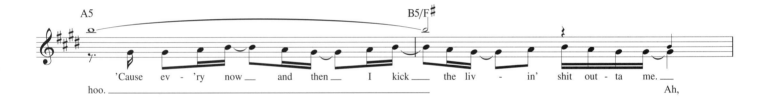

A5   B5/F♯

'Cause ev - 'ry now __ and then __ I kick __ the liv - in' shit out - ta me. __
hoo. _____ Ah,

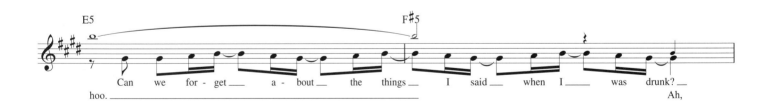

E5   F♯5

Can we for - get __ a - bout __ the things __ I said __ when I __ was drunk? __
hoo. _____ Ah,

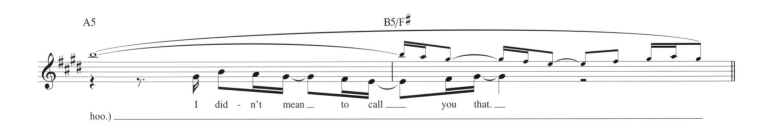

A5   B5/F♯

I did - n't mean __ to call __ you that. __
hoo.) _____

Outro

Gtrs. 1 & 2: w/ Rhy. Figs. 1 & 1A

E5   B5 A5   E5   B5   A5

One Step Closer

Words and Music by Rob Bourdon, Brad Delson, Joe Hahn, Mike Shinoda and Charles Bennington

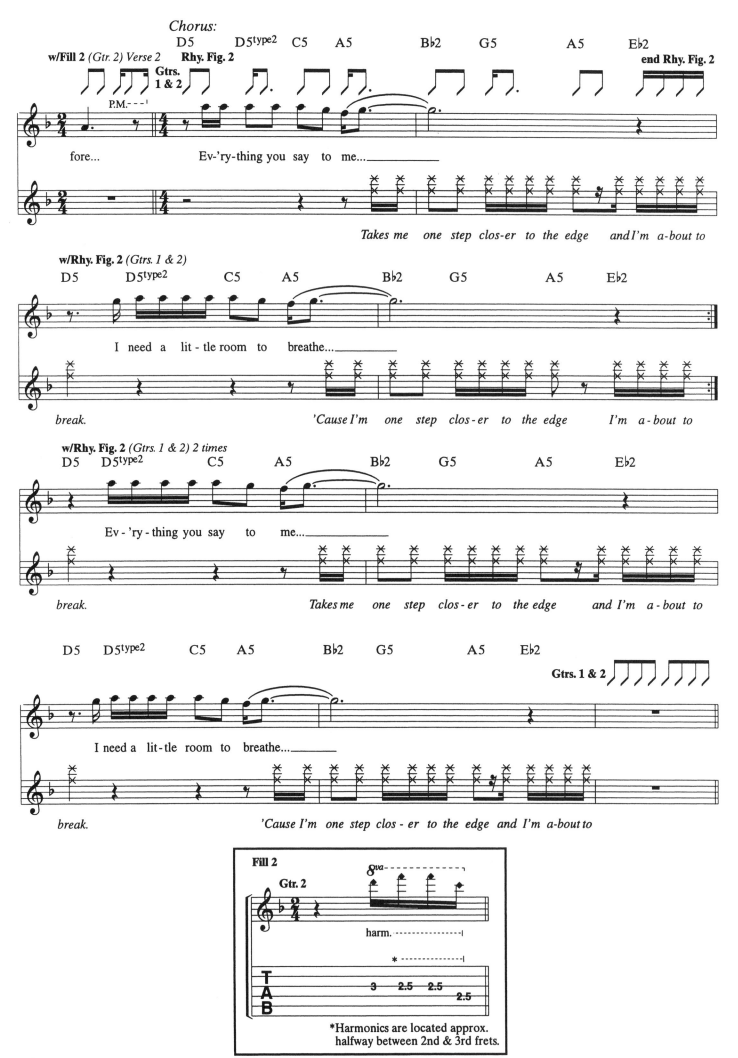

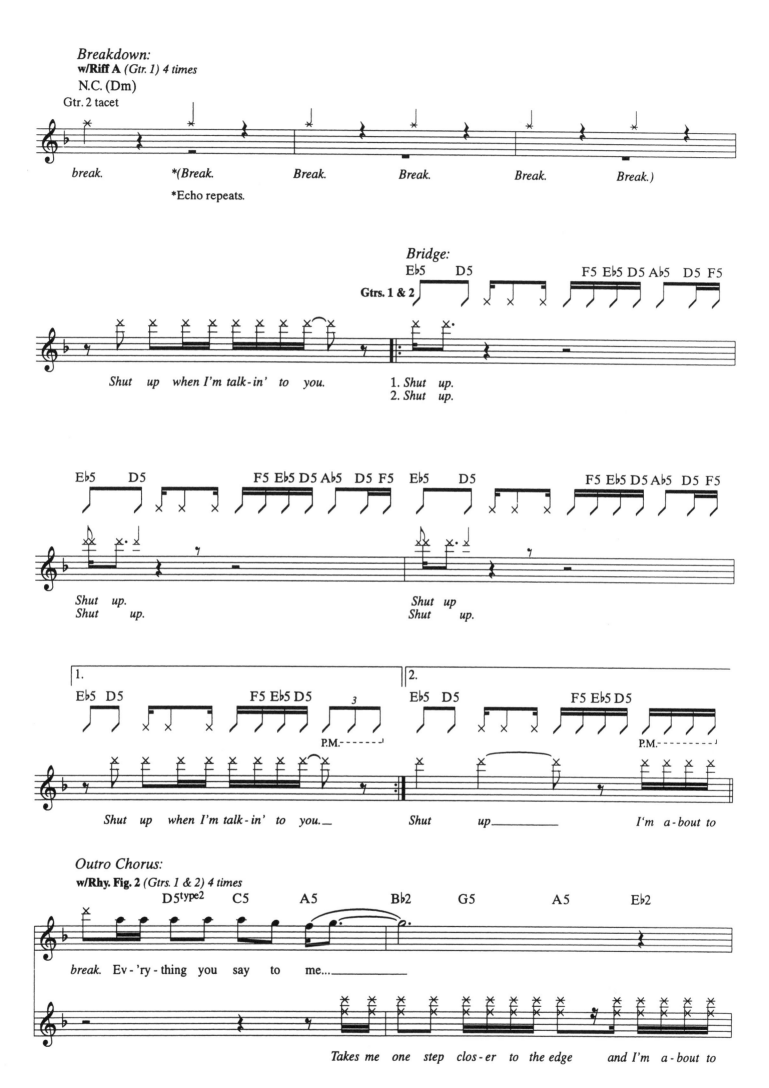

I need a lit-tle room to breathe..._____

break.   'Cause I'm one step clos-er to the edge;   I'm a-bout to

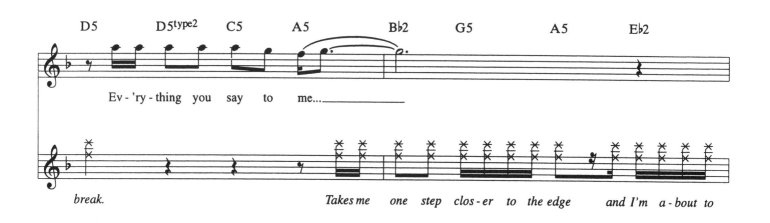

Ev-'ry-thing you say to me..._____

break.   Takes me one step clos-er to the edge   and I'm a-bout to

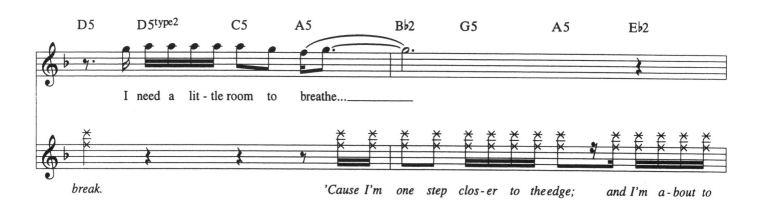

I need a lit-tle room to breathe..._____

break.   'Cause I'm one step clos-er to the edge;   and I'm a-bout to

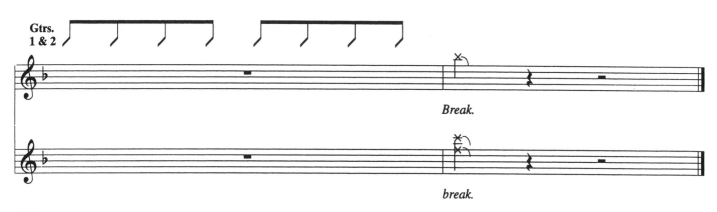

Break.

break.

One Way or Another

Words and Music by Deborah Harry and Nigel Harrison

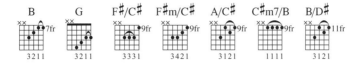

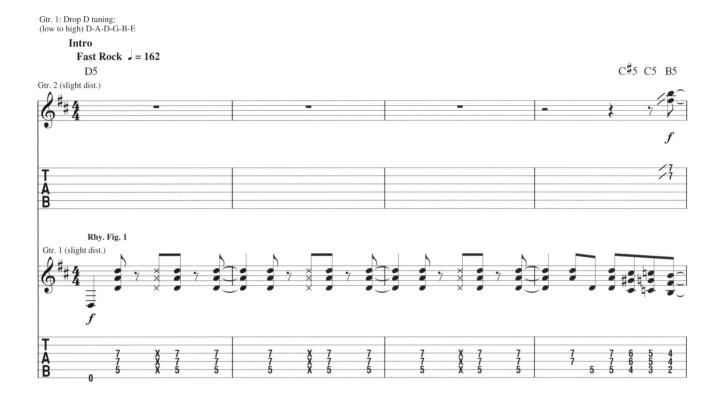

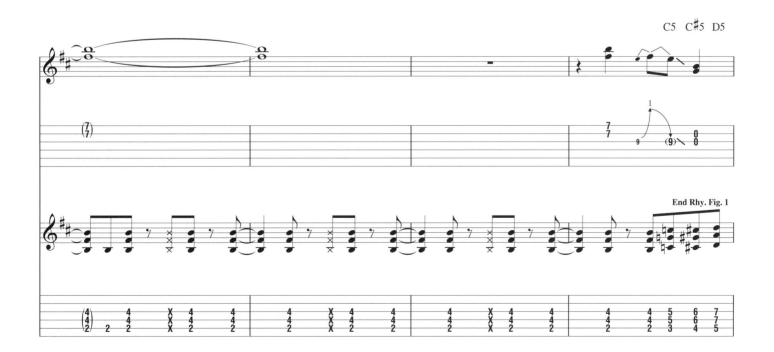

Gtr. 1: w/ Rhy. Fig. 1

D

C#5 C5 B5

B

C5 C#5 D5

End Rhy. Fig. 2

Verse
Gtr. 1: w/ Rhy. Fig. 1 (1 3/4 times)
Gtr. 2: w/ Riff A
Gtr. 3: w/ Rhy. Fig. 2 (1 3/4 times)

D

C#5 C5 B5

1. One way or an - oth - er, I'm gon - na find ya. I'm gon - na get ya, get ya, get ya, get ya.

B

C5 C#5 D5

One way __ or an - oth - er, I'm gon - na win ya. I'm gon - na get ya, get ya, get ya, get ya.

176

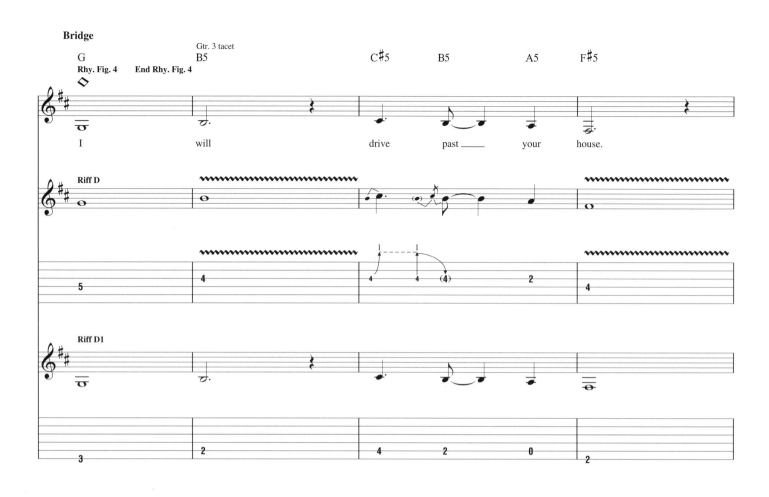

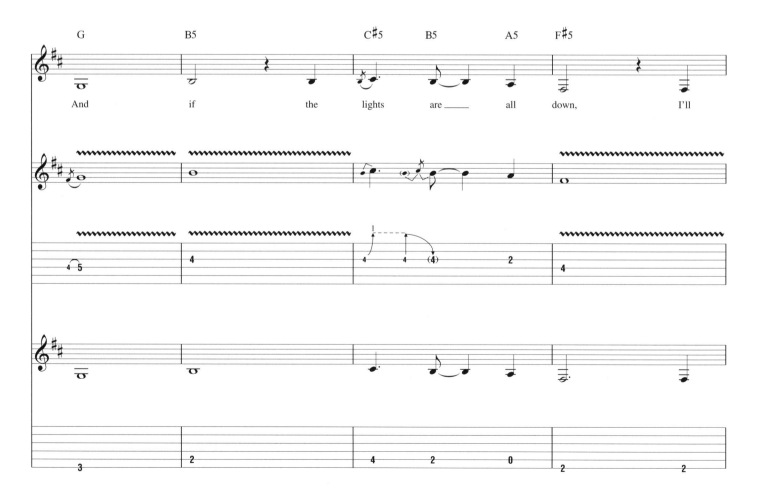

*Editors note: To avoid clash between A♮ (played by Gtr. 4) and A♯ (the Major 3rd in the F♯/C♯ chord) substitute F♯m/C♯.   **As before.

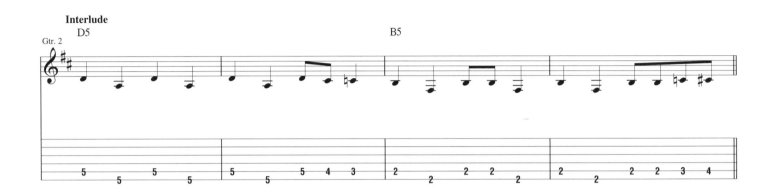

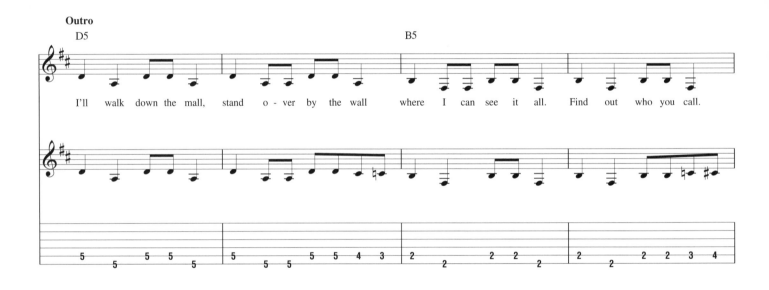

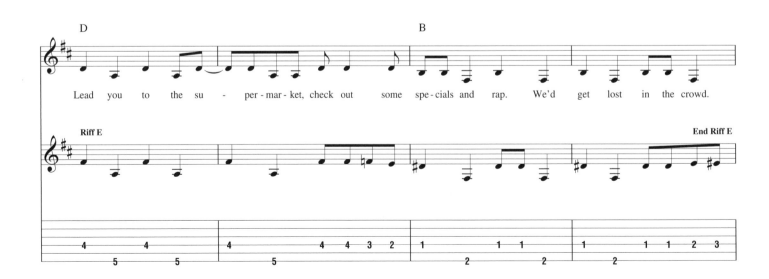

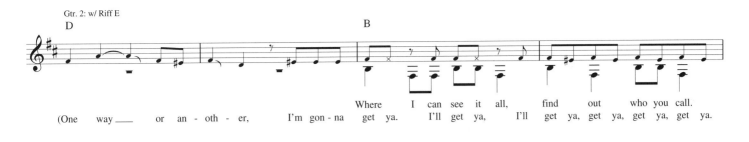

(One way ___ or an - oth - er, I'm gon - na get ya. I'll get ya, I'll get ya, get ya, get ya, get ya.

One way ___ or an - oth - er, I'm gon - na get ya. I'll get ya, I'll get ya, get ya, get ya, get ya.

One way ___ or an - oth - er, I'm gon - na get ya. I'll get ya, I'll get ya, get ya, get ya, get ya.

*Two synths. arr. for gtr.

One way ___ or an - oth - er, I'm gon - na get ya. I'll get ya, I'll get ya, get ya, get ya, get ya.)

Peace Sells

Words and Music by Dave Mustaine

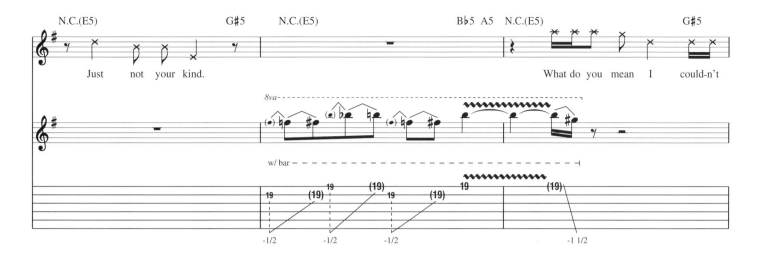

Just not your kind. What do you mean I could-n't

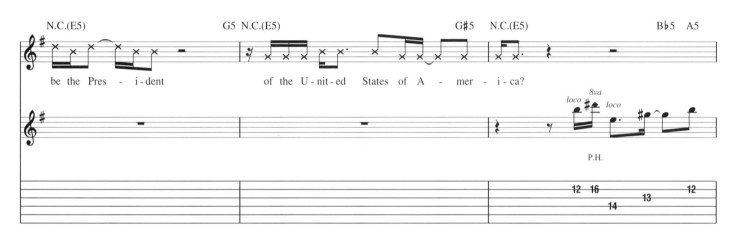

be the Pres - i - dent of the U - nit - ed States of A - mer - i - ca?

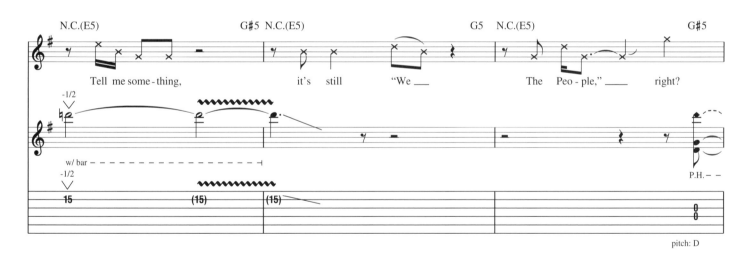

Tell me some-thing, it's still "We ___ The Peo - ple," ___ right?

pitch: D

Chorus

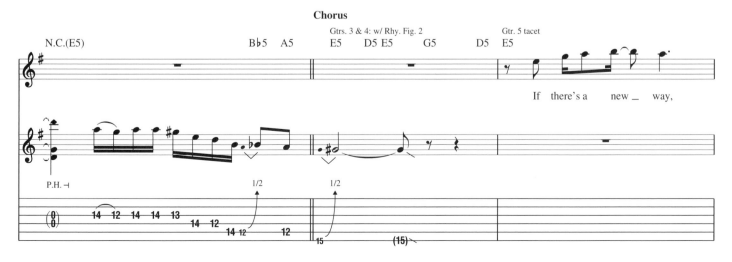

If there's a new ___ way,

well, I'll be the first __ in line. __

But it bet-ter work this time. __

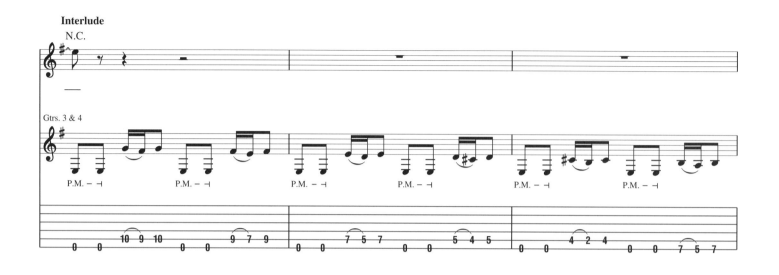

Interlude

* P.M. applies to both gtrs., next 4 meas.

Guitar Solo

Oh. _____

fdbk.

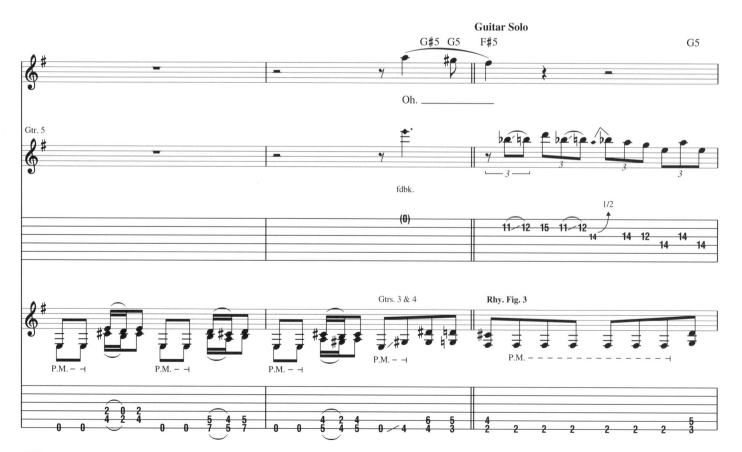

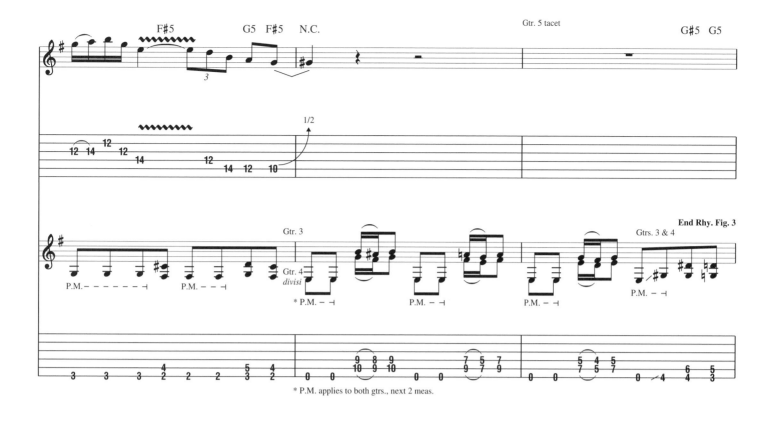

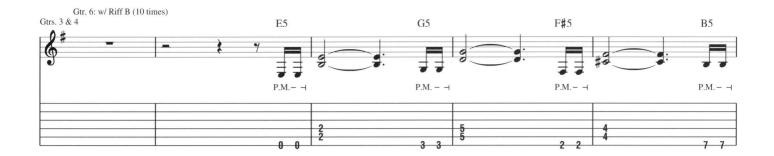

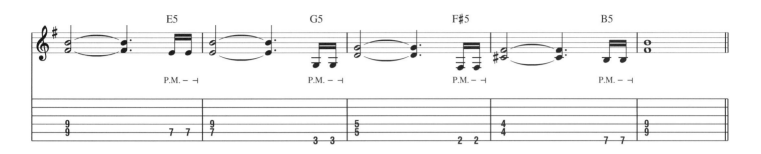

Bridge

Gtr. 6 tacet

* Chord symbols implied by bass, till Outro.

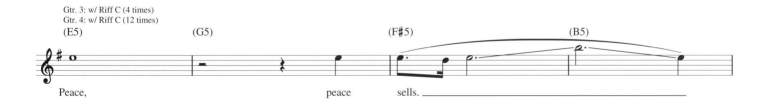

Gtr. 3: w/ Riff D (4 times)

Peace sells, but who's buy-ing? Peace sells, but who's buy-ing?

Guitar Solo

Gtrs. 3 & 4: w/ Riff C (8 times)

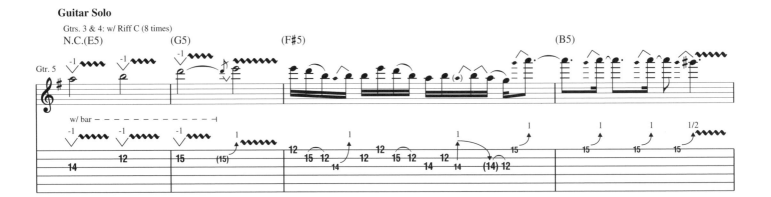

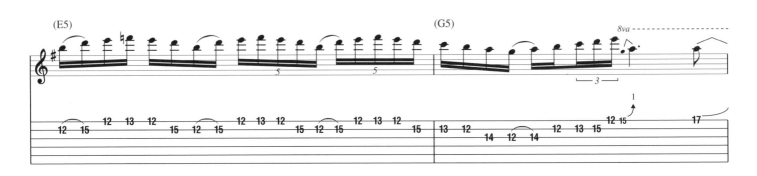

Bridge

Gtr. 3: w/ Riff D (8 times)
Gtr. 4: w/ Riff C (14 times)
Gtr. 5 tacet

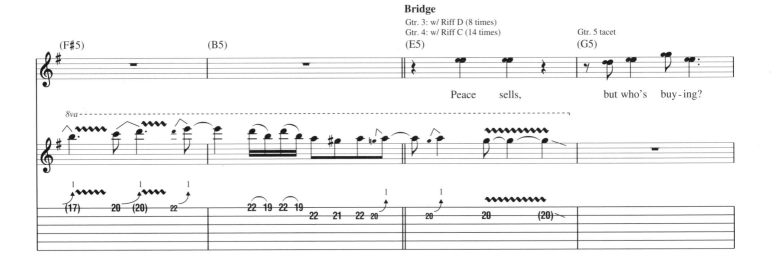

Peace sells, but who's buy-ing?

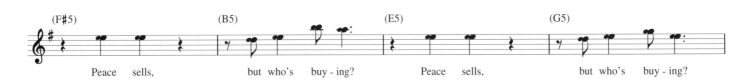

Peace sells, but who's buy-ing? Peace sells, but who's buy-ing?

Gtr. 3: w/ Riff C (6 times)

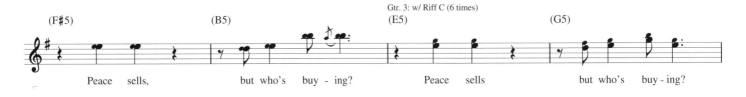

Peace sells, but who's buy-ing? Peace sells but who's buy-ing?

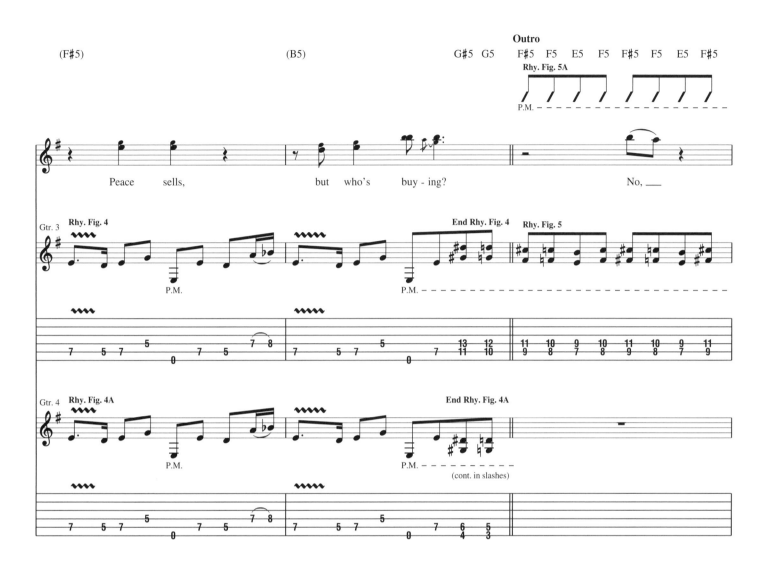

Pinball Wizard

Words and Music by Pete Townshend

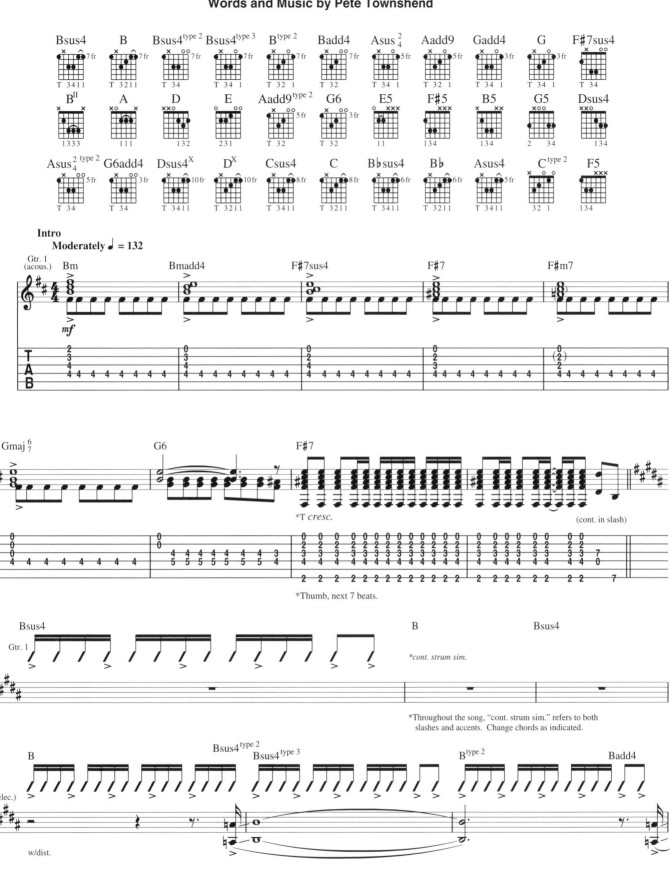

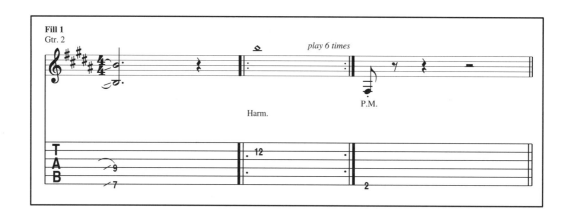

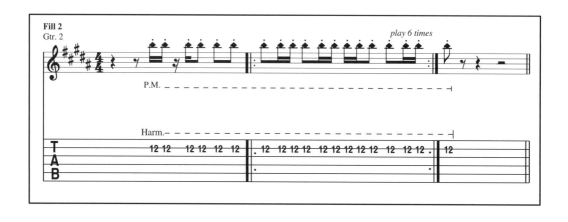

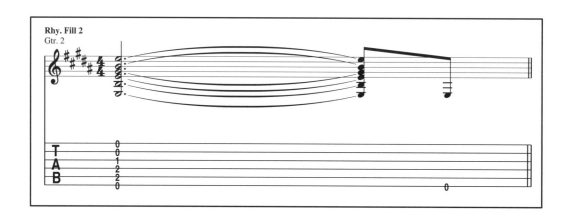

Ramblin' Man

Words and Music by Dickey Betts

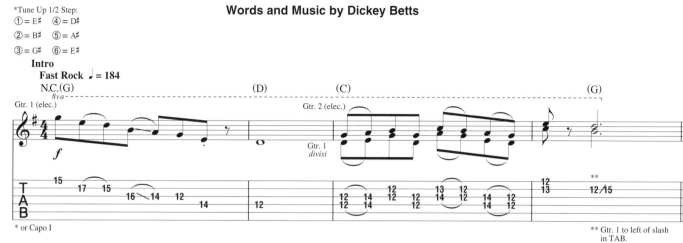

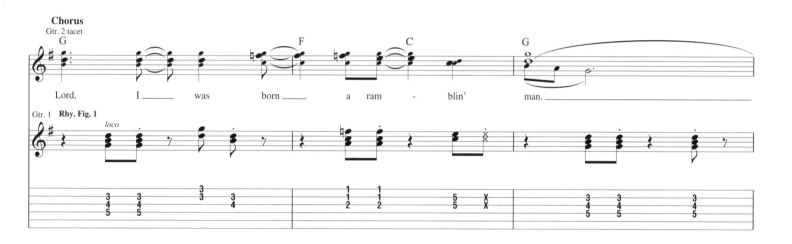

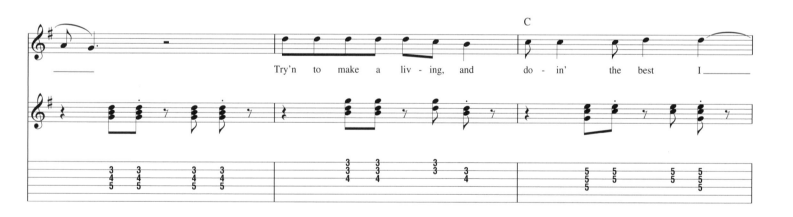

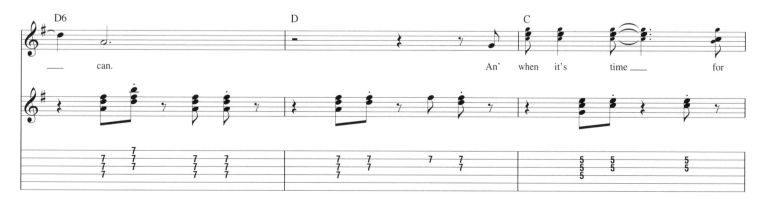

Interlude

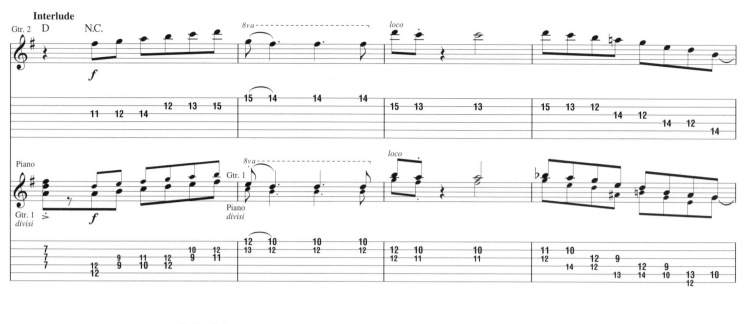

Guitar Solo

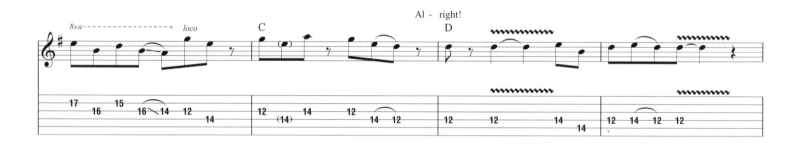

* Gtr. 1 to left of slash in TAB.

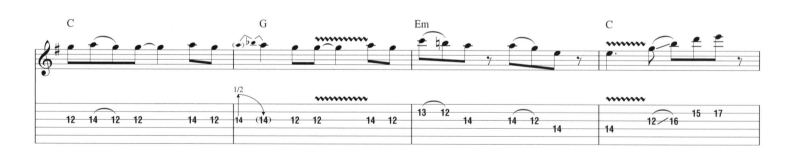

Al - right!

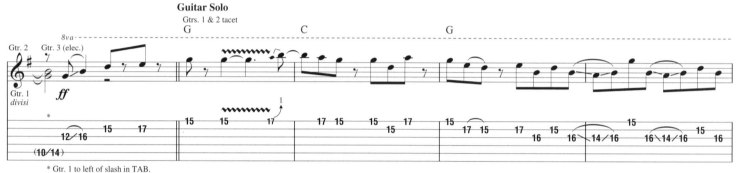

D.S. al Coda

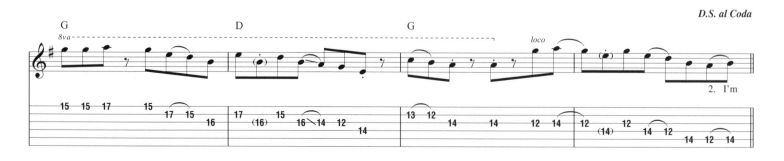

2. I'm

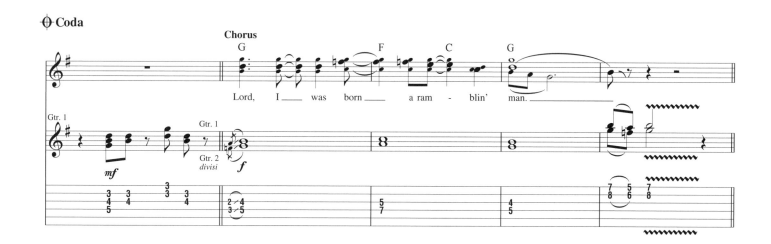

Coda

Chorus

Lord, I ___ was born ___ a ram - blin' man. ___

Gtr. 1

Gtr. 1
Gtr. 2 *divisi*

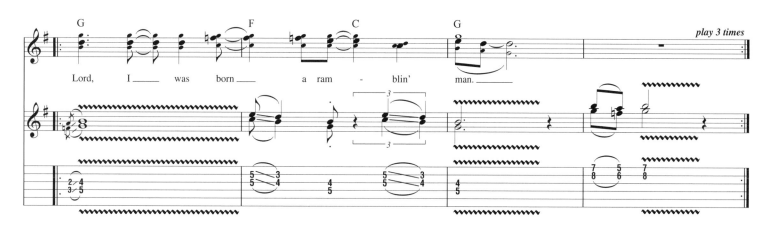

Lord, I ___ was born ___ a ram - blin' man. ___

play 3 times

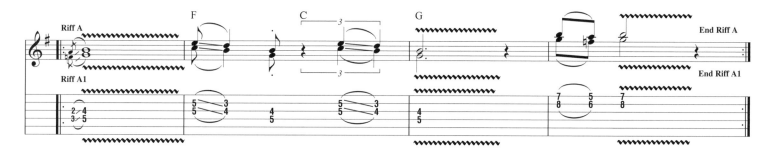

Riff A

End Riff A

Riff A1

End Riff A1

* Gtrs. 1 & 2: w/ Riffs A & A1

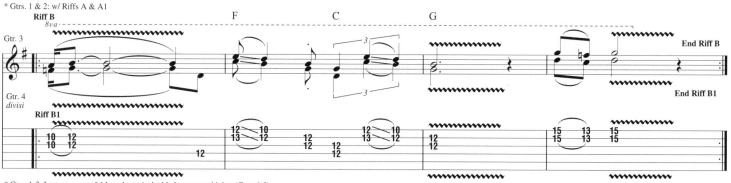

Riff B
8va

Gtr. 3

End Riff B

Gtr. 4
divisi

End Riff B1

Riff B1

* Gtrs. 1-3: Last measure of 4 bar phrase is doubled an octave higher (Gtrs. 6-8)

Guitar Solo

Gtr. 5 ** Gtrs. 1-4: w/ Riffs A, A1, B & B1, till fade
(elec.)

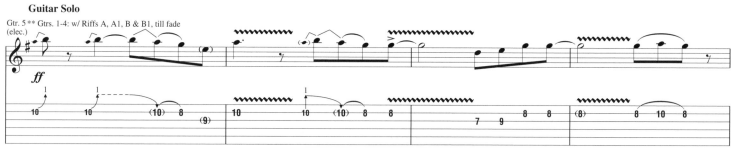

ff

** Gtrs. 6-8 cont. simile, till fade.

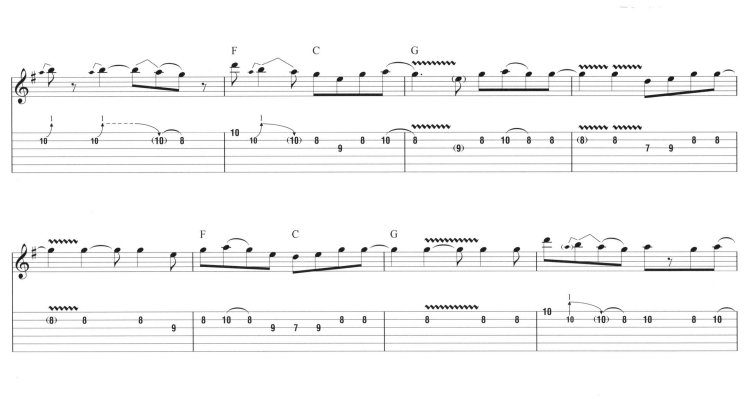

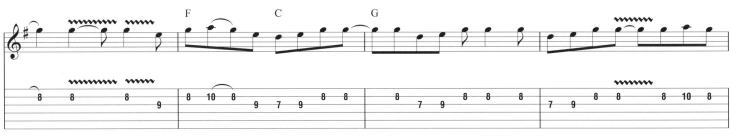

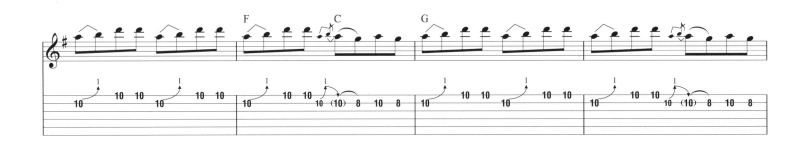

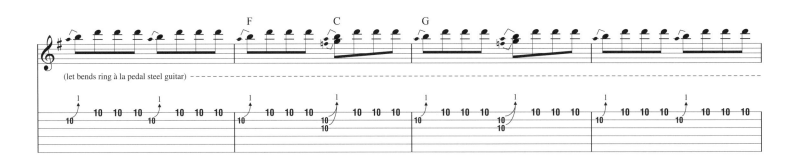

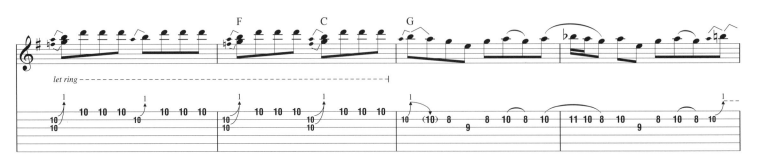

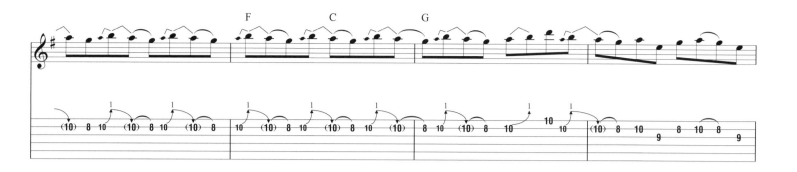

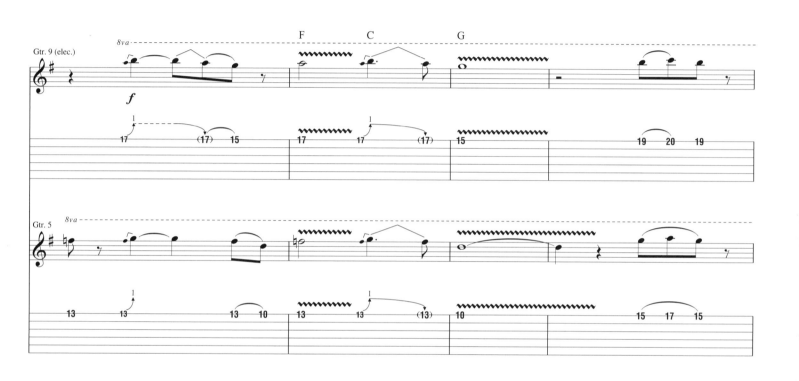

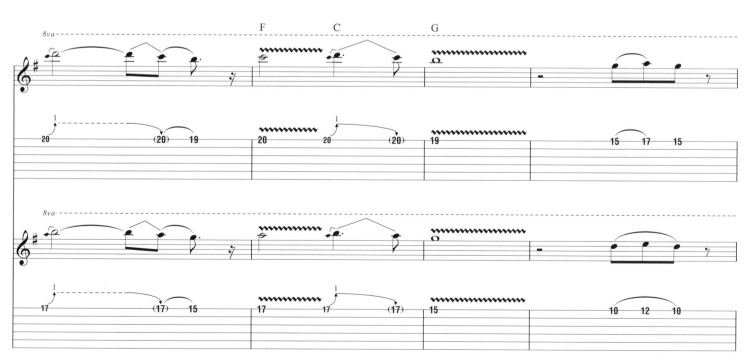

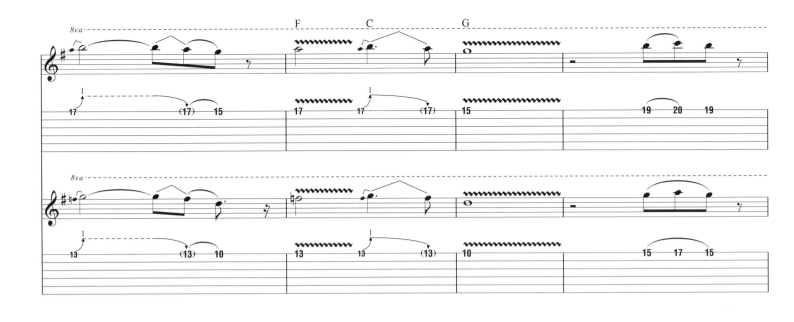

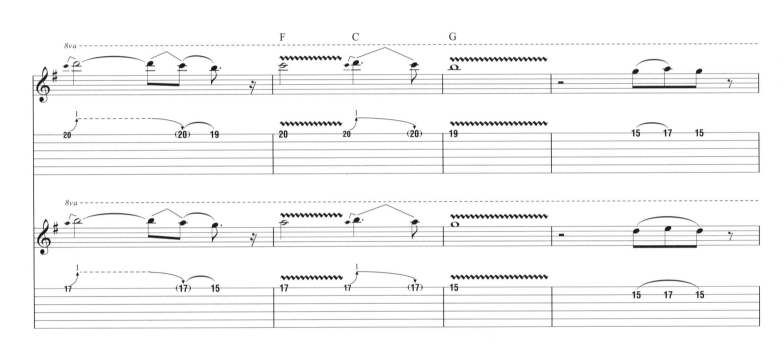

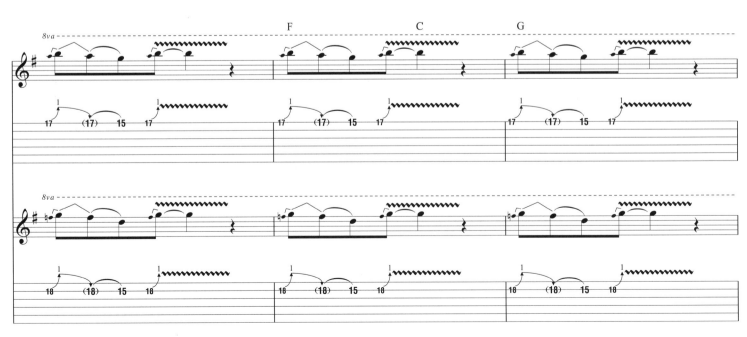

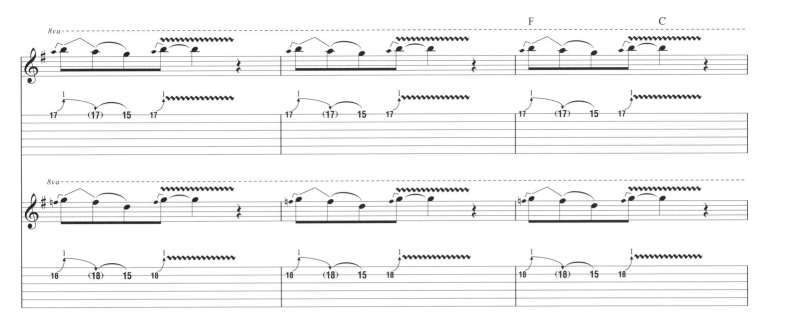

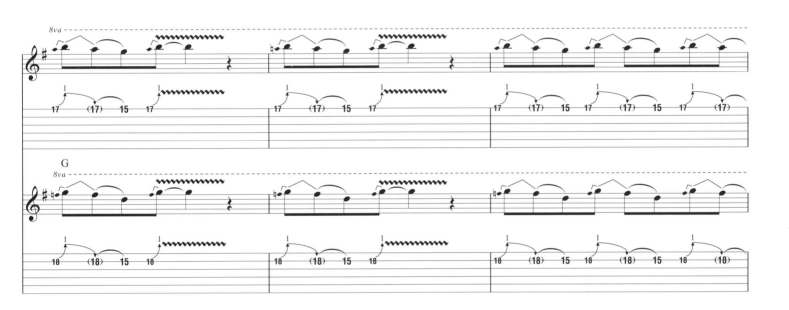

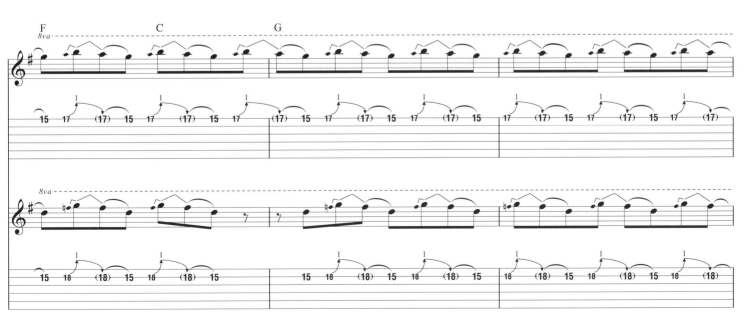

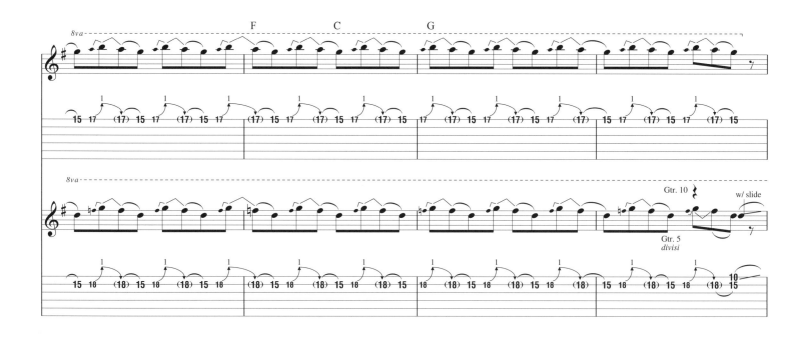

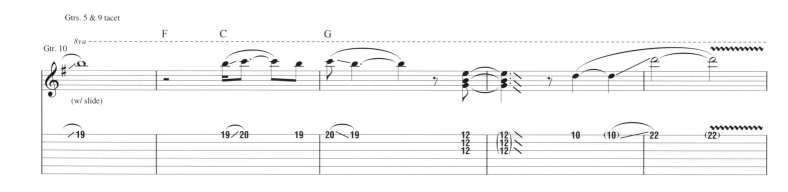

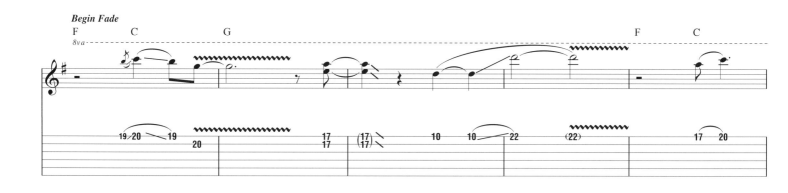

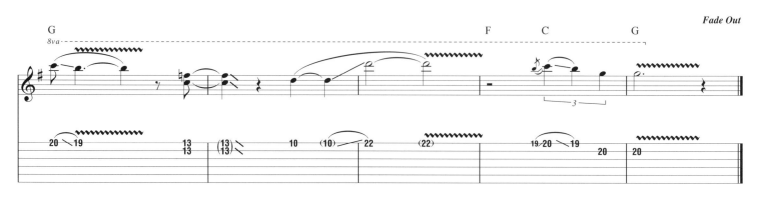

Rock'n Me

Words and Music by Steve Miller

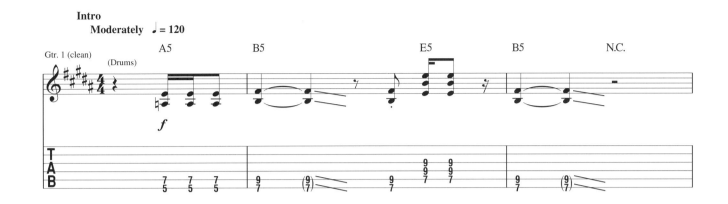

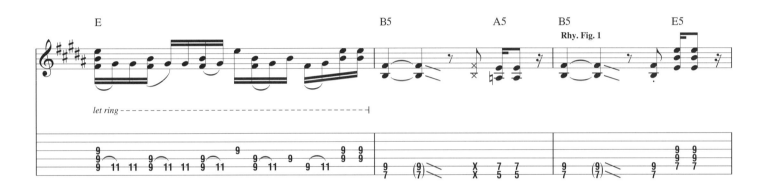

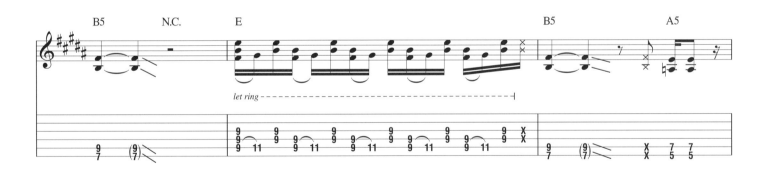

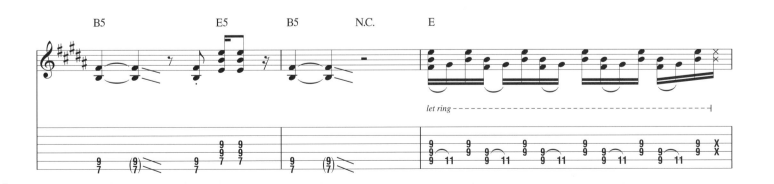

woman is a friend of mine.____ And I know____ that it's true____ that all the
del - phi - a, At - lan - ta, L. A.____ North - ern Cal - i - for - nia where the

To Coda ⊕

things that I do will come back____ to me in my sweet-n time._____ So keep on
girls are warm,__ so I could hear my sweet, mm, ba - by say.____ Keep on a

Chorus

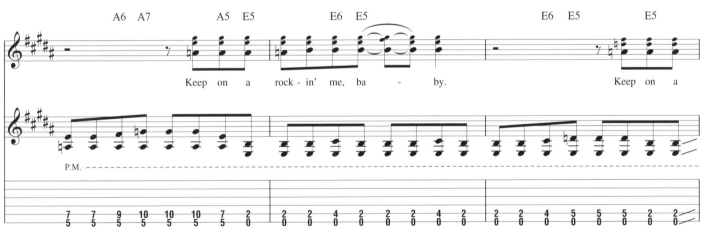

rock - in' me, ba - by. Keep on a rock - in' me, ba - by.

Keep on a rock - in' me, ba - by. Keep on a

Verse

Gtr. 1: w/ Rhy. Fig. 2

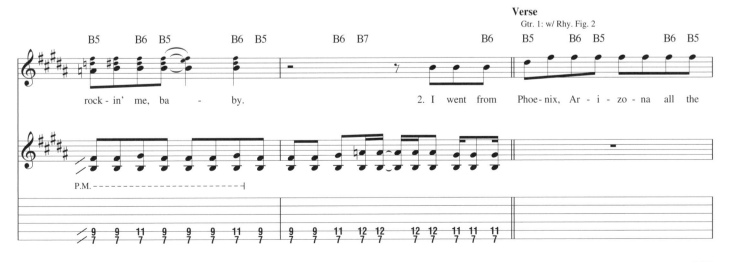

rock - in' me, ba - by. 2. I went from Phoe - nix, Ar - i - zo - na all the

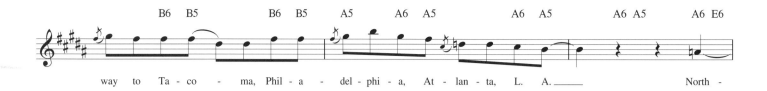

way to Ta-co-ma, Phil-a-del-phi-a, At-lan-ta, L. A._____ North-

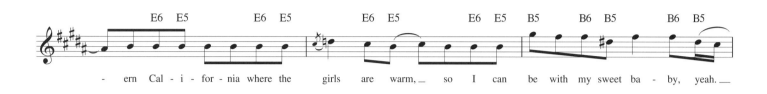

-ern Cal-i-for-nia where the girls are warm,__ so I can be with my sweet ba-by, yeah.__

Chorus

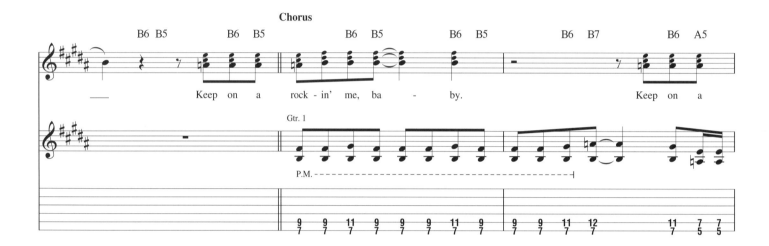

_____ Keep on a rock-in' me, ba - by. Keep on a

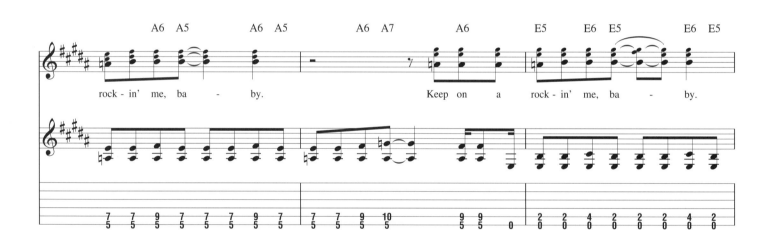

rock-in' me, ba - by. Keep on a rock-in' me, ba - by.

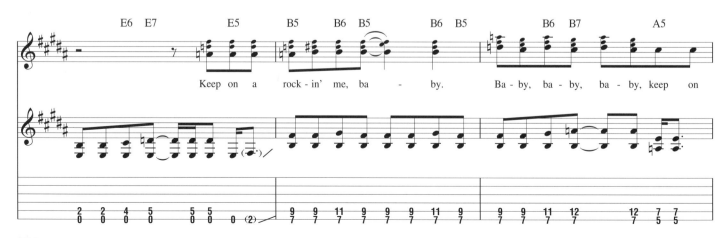

Keep on a rock-in' me, ba - by. Ba-by, ba-by, ba-by, keep on

Round and Round

Words and Music by Robbin Lantz Crosby, Warren DeMartini and Stephen E. Pearcy

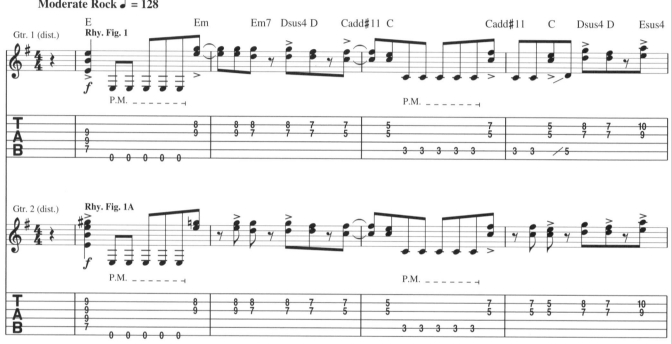

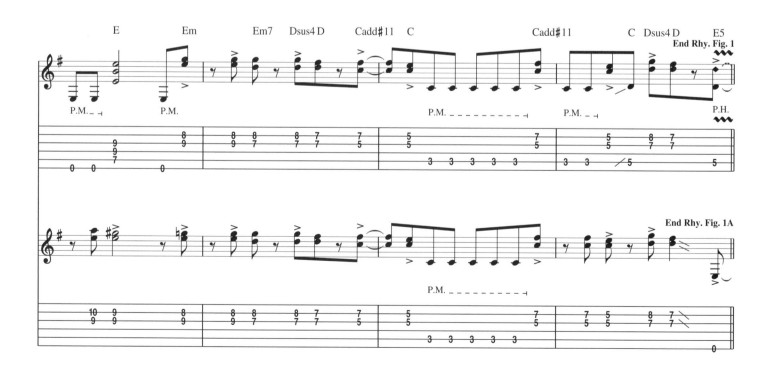

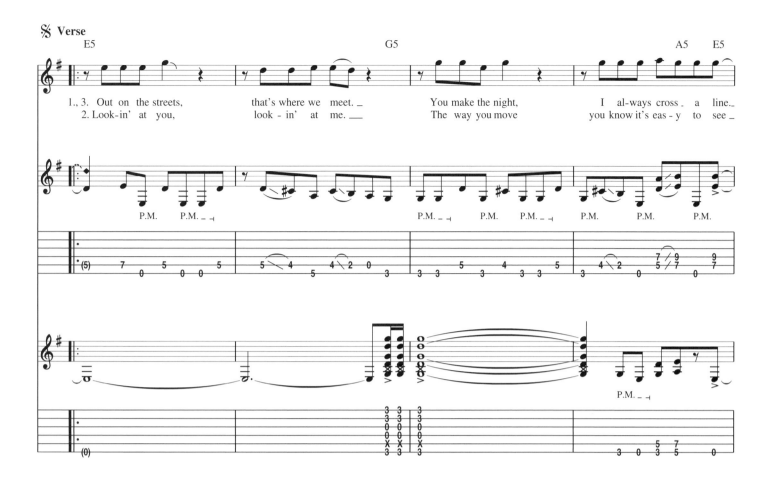

1., 3. Out on the streets,   that's where we meet. __   You make the night,   I al-ways cross __ a line. __
2. Look-in' at you,   look - in' at me. __   The way you move   you know it's eas - y to see __

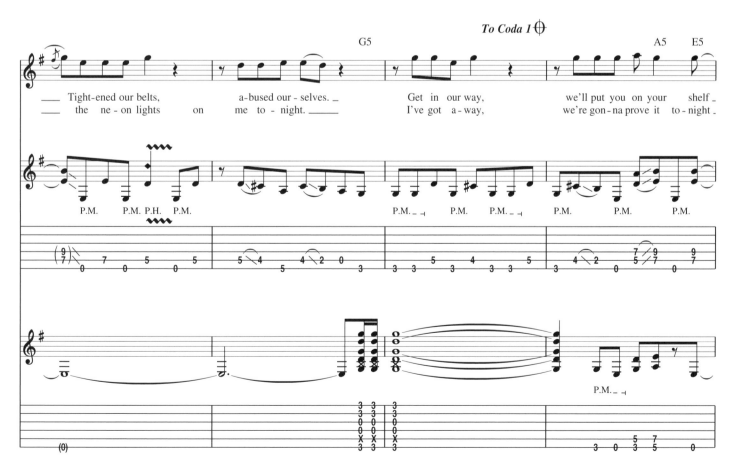

To Coda 1

____ Tight-ened our belts,   a-bused our - selves. __   Get in our way,   we'll put you on your   shelf __
____ the ne - on lights   on   me to - night. ____   I've got a - way,   we're gon-na prove it   to - night __

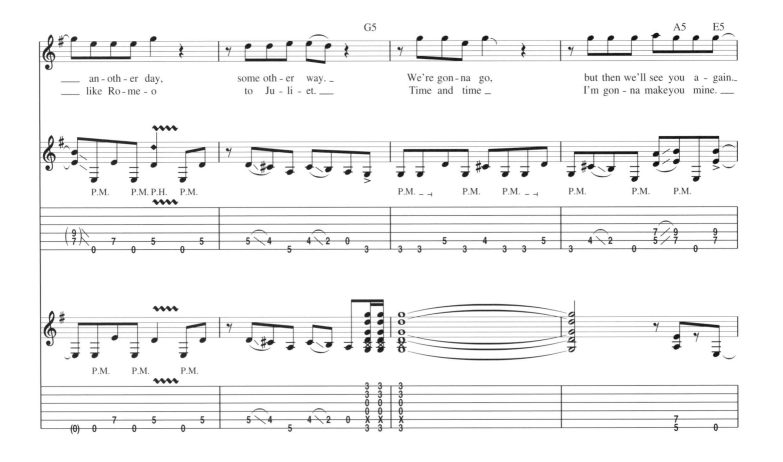

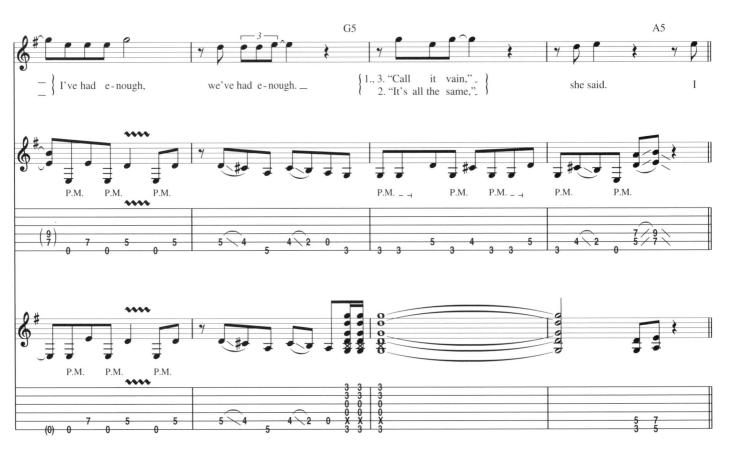

Pre-Chorus

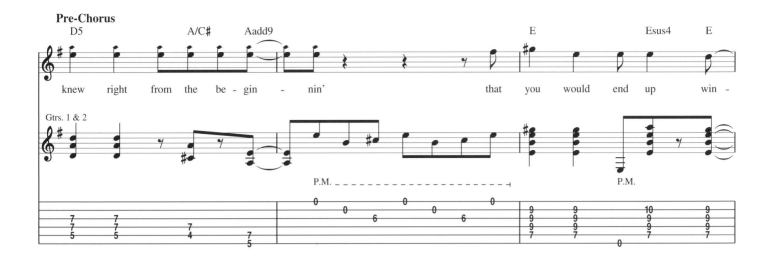

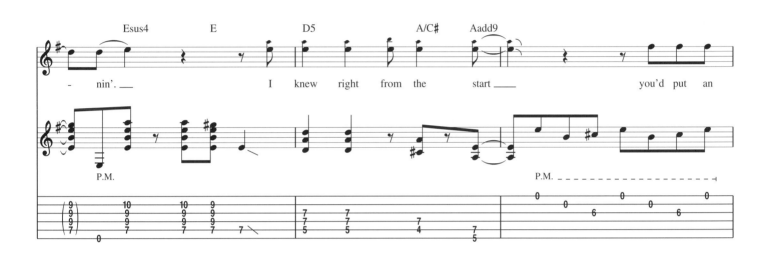

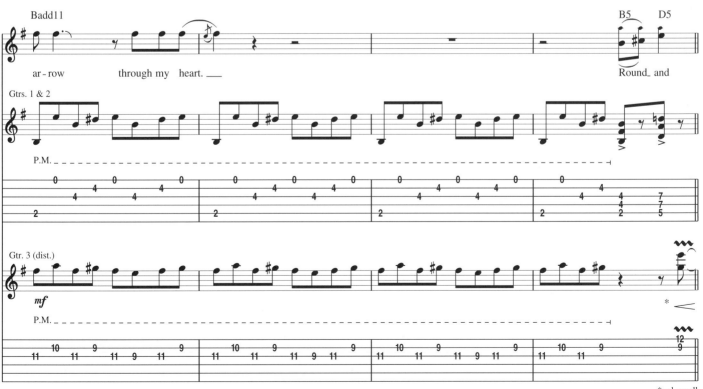

*vol. swell

𝄋 𝄋 Chorus

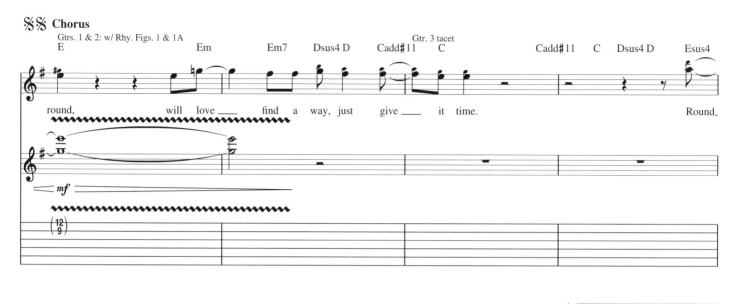

round, will love ___ find a way, just give ___ it time. Round ___

___ and round, what comes ___ a-round goes a-round. I'll tell you why. Dig!

Guitar Solo

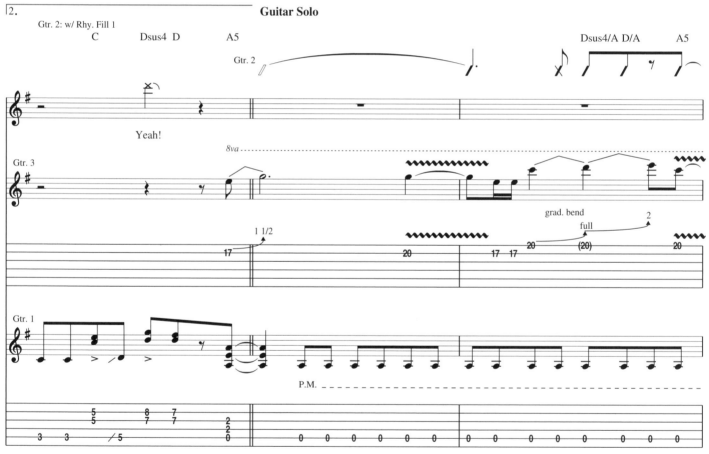

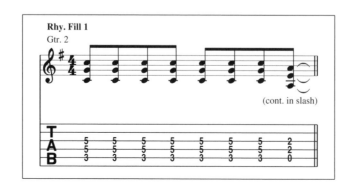

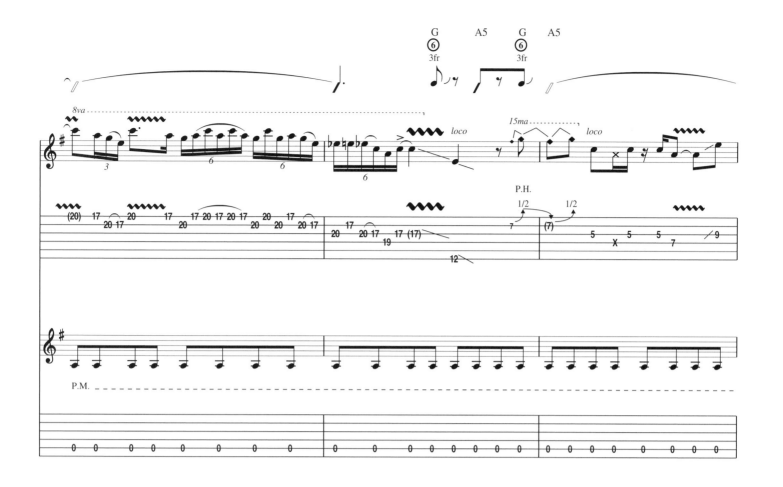

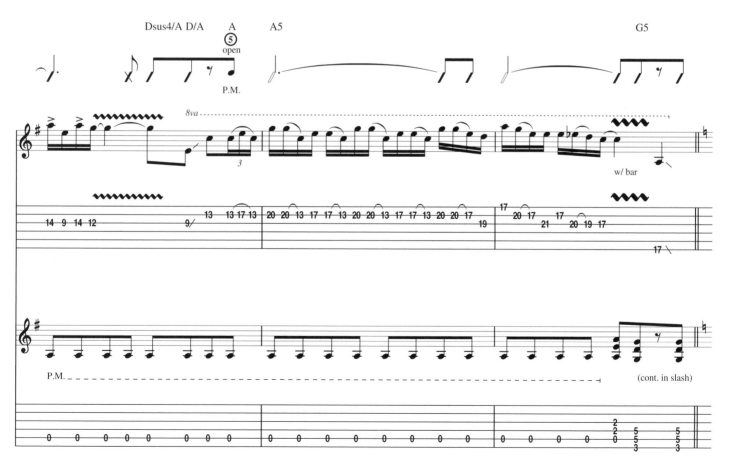

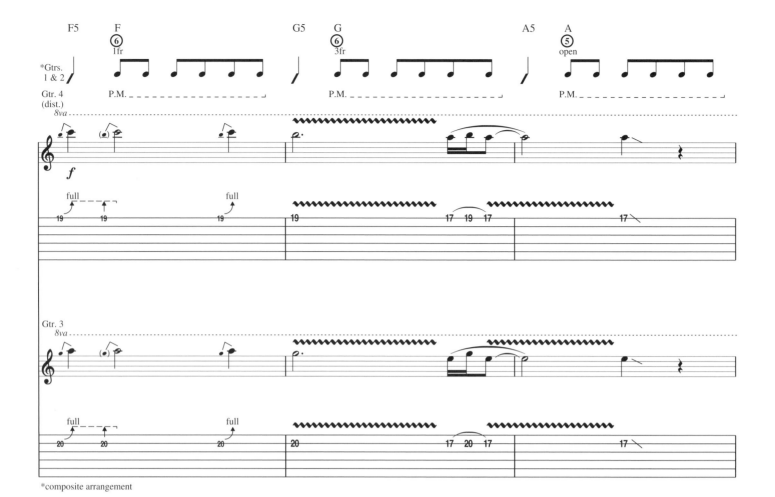

*composite arrangement

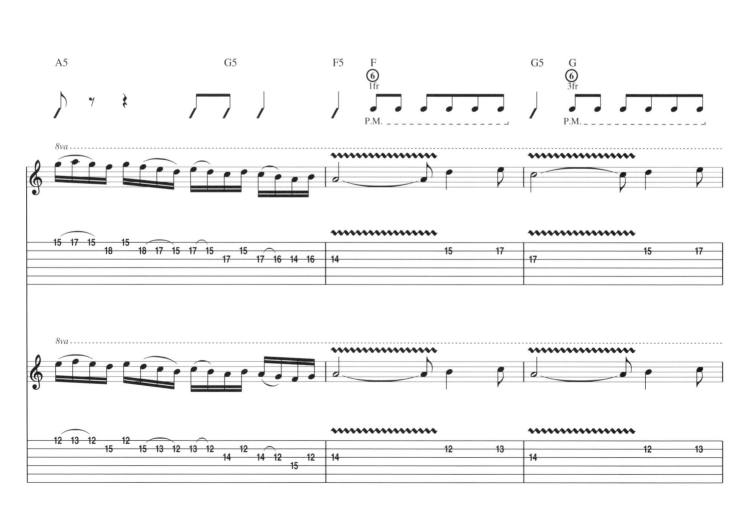

Outro-Guitar Solo

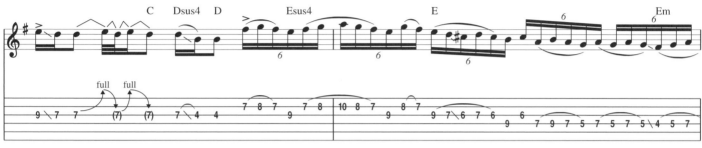

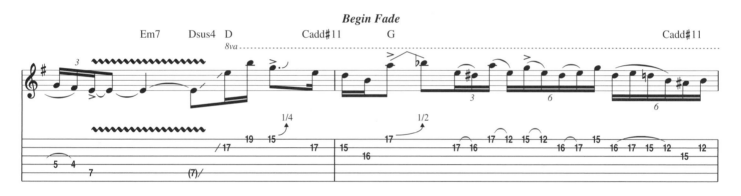

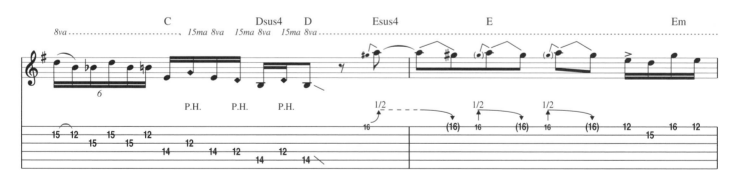

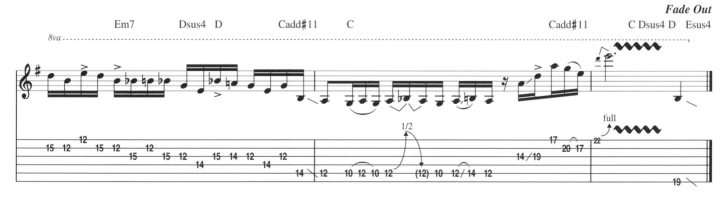

Shooting Star

Words and Music by Paul Rodgers

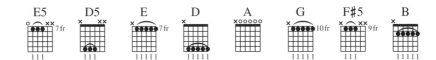

Gtr. 3; Open A Tuning:
① = E ④ = E
② = C♯ ⑤ = A
③ = A ⑥ = E

* Chord symbols reflect basic tonality.

* Two gtrs. arr. for one

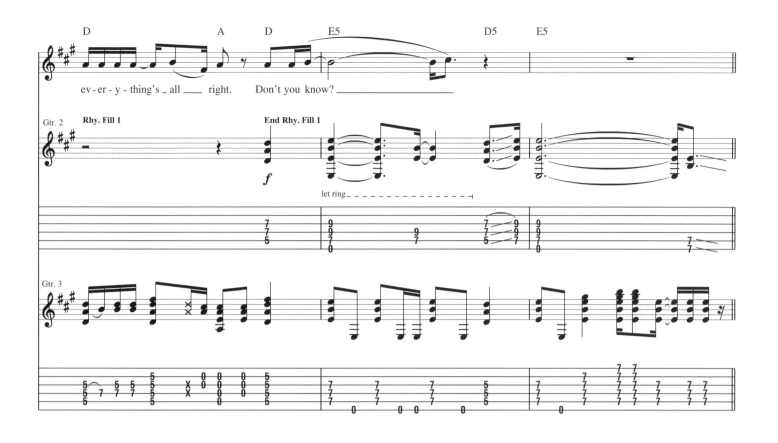

ev - er - y - thing's _ all ___ right. Don't you know? ___

Verse

Gtr. 3: w/ Rhy. Fig. 1, simile
Gtr. 2 tacet

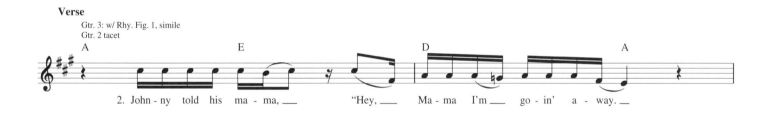

2. John - ny told his ma - ma, ___ "Hey, ___ Ma - ma I'm ___ go - in' a - way.

I'm gon - na hit the big time, ___ gon - na be a big star some - day," ___ yeah. _

Gtr. 3: w/ Rhy. Fig. 2, 1 1/2 times, simile

Ma - ma came to the door _ with a tear - drop in her eye. _ John - ny said, "Don't _ cry, ma - ma,

Chorus

Gtrs. 2 & 3: w/ Rhy. Figs. 3 & 3A, simile

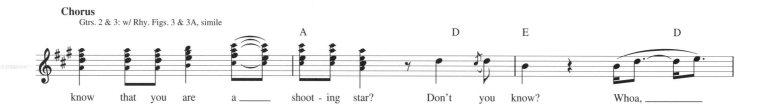

know that you are a _____ shoot - ing star? Don't you know? Whoa, _____

yeah. _____ Don't you _____ know that you are a _____ shoot - ing star? _____ Yeah. _ And all _

_____ the world _ will love _ you _ just as long, _____ as long as you are _____ a shoot - ing

Guitar Solo

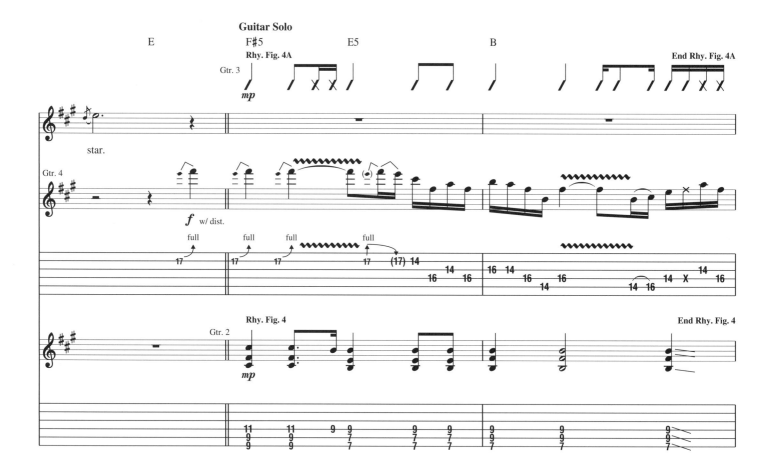

star.

Gtrs. 2 & 3: w/ Rhy. Figs. 4 & 4A, 2 times

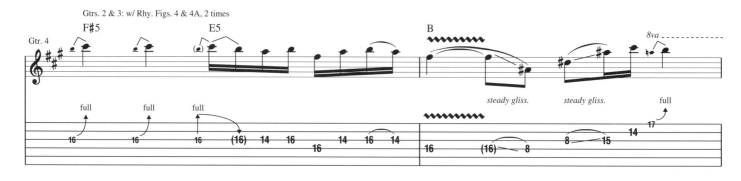

* Played behind the beat.

D.S. al Coda

Don't you.____

4. John - ny died one ___ night, ___ died in his bed. ___

Bot-tle of whis-key, sleep-ing tab - lets by his head. ___ John-ny's life passed him by ___ like a

warm sum - mer day. ___ If you lis - ten to the wind you ___ can ___

Spirit in the Sky

Words and Music by Norman Greenbaum

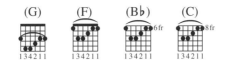

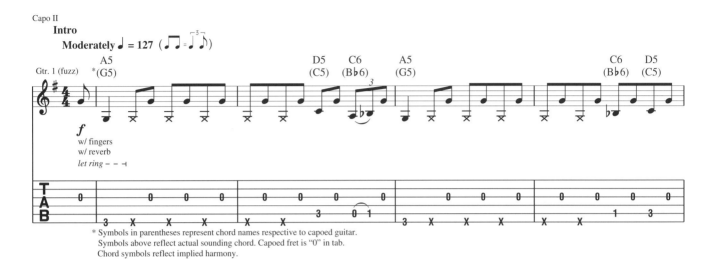

* Symbols in parentheses represent chord names respective to capoed guitar.
Symbols above reflect actual sounding chord. Capoed fret is "0" in tab.
Chord symbols reflect implied harmony.

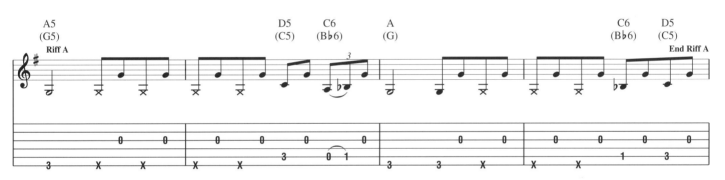

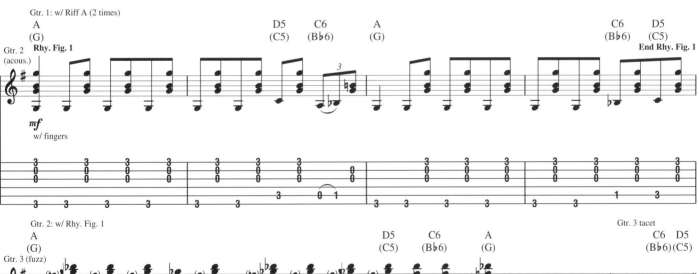

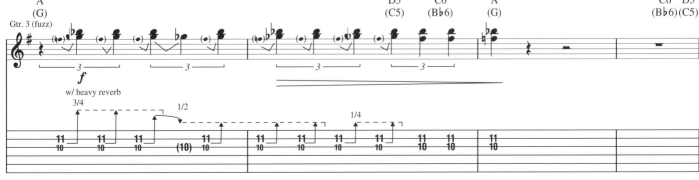

Verse

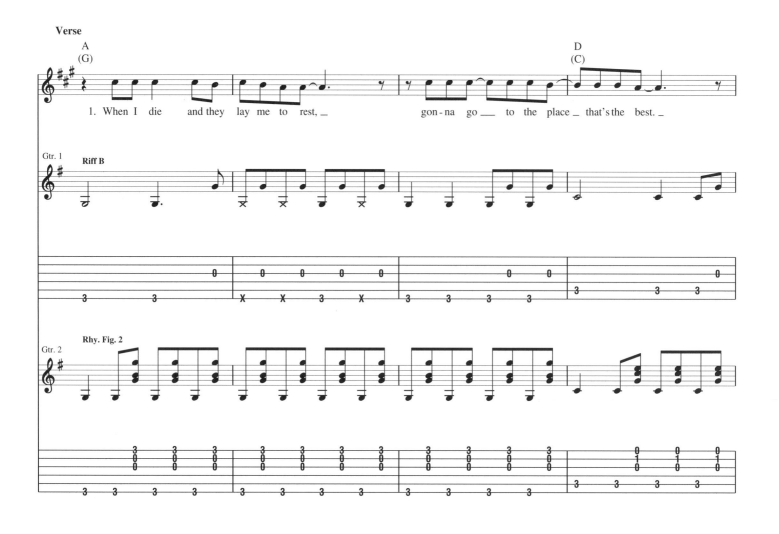

1. When I die and they lay me to rest, ___ gon-na go ___ to the place ___ that's the best. ___

When I lay me down ___ to die, ___ go-in' up ___ to the Spir-it in the Sky.

let ring -

Verse

Gtr. 1: w/ Riff B
Gtr. 2: w/ Rhy. Fig. 2

A
(G)

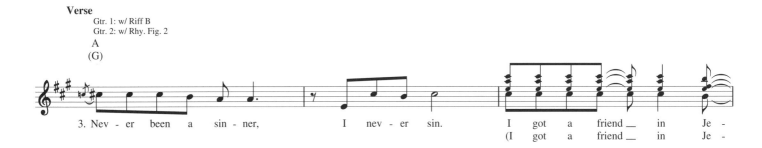

3. Nev - er been a sin - ner, I nev - er sin. I got a friend ___ in Je -
(I got a friend ___ in Je -

D   A
(C)   (G)

- sus, _____ so you know that when I die ___ He's
- sus.) _____

Chorus

Gtr. 1: w/ Riff C, 1st 6 meas.
Gtr. 2: w/ Rhy. Fig. 2, 1st 6 meas.

E   A   A
(D)   (G)   (G)

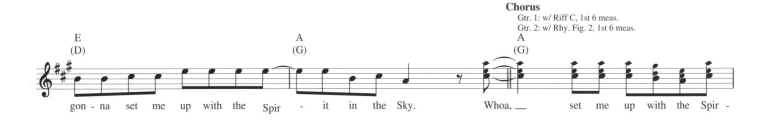

gon - na set me up with the Spir - it in the Sky. Whoa, ___ set me up with the Spir -

D
(C)

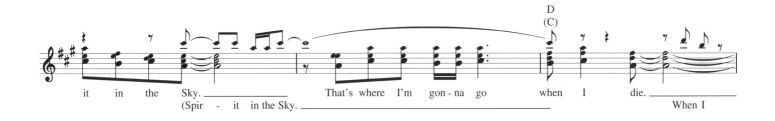

it in the Sky. _____ That's where I'm gon - na go when I die. _____
(Spir - it in the Sky. _____ When I

Gtrs. 1 & 2: w/ Rhy. Fills 1 & 1A (2 times)

A   E
(G)   (D)

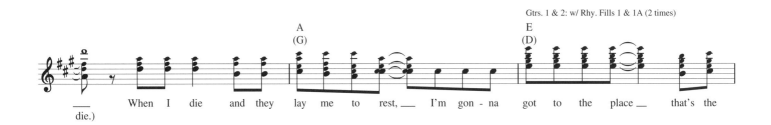

___ When I die and they lay me to rest, ___ I'm gon - na got to the place ___ that's the
die.)

Interlude

Gtr. 1: w/ Riff A (2 times)
Gtr. 2: w/ Rhy. Fig. 1 (2 times)

A   E   A   A   D5 C6
(G)   (D)   (G)   (G)   (C5)(Bb6)

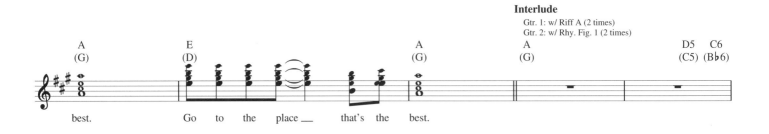

best. Go to the place ___ that's the best.

Gtr. 3: w/ Riff E   Gtr. 3: w/ Riff D
A   C6 D5 A   D5 C6 A   C6 D5
(G)   (Bb6)(C5)(G)   (C5)(Bb6)(G)   (Bb6)(C5)

240

Outro Guitar Solo

Gtr. 1: w/ Riff A (4 times)
Gtr. 2: w/ Rhy. Fig. 1 (4 times)

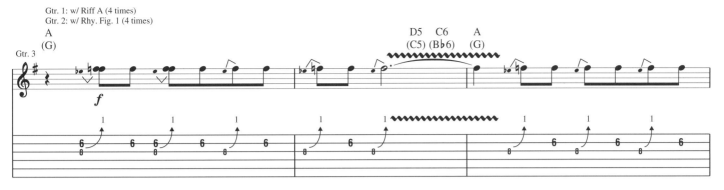

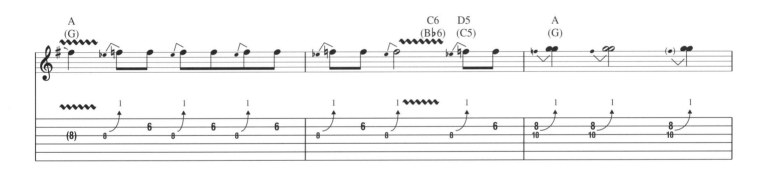

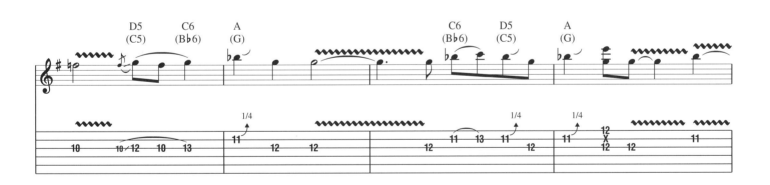

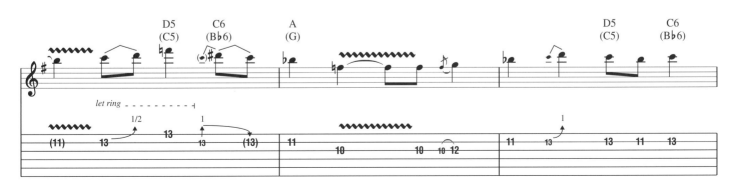

Spoonman

Words and Music by Chris Cornell

The Trees

Words by Neil Peart
Music by Geddy Lee and Alex Lifeson

Ma-ples want more sun-light and the Oaks ig-nore their pleas.

(Gtr. I out)

*Gtr. II **

*Elec. w/dist. (doubled throughout).

**Play only lowest strings of chords
on eight notes (next 4 bars).

2. The

248

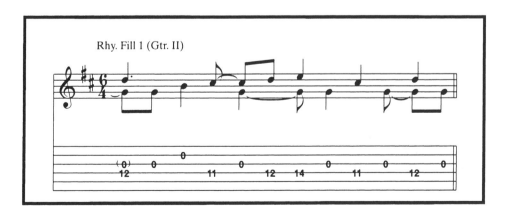

*Play only lowest strings of chords
on eight notes (next 4 bars).

trees are all kept e - qual by hatch-et,

axe, and saw.

We Got the Beat

Words and Music by Charlotte Caffey

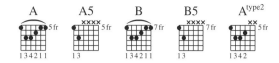

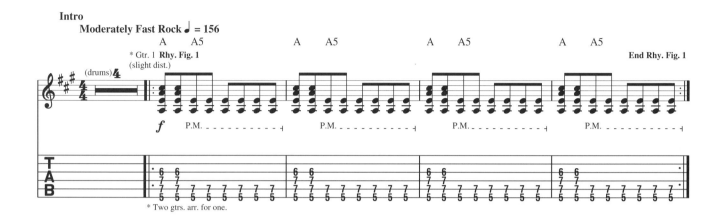

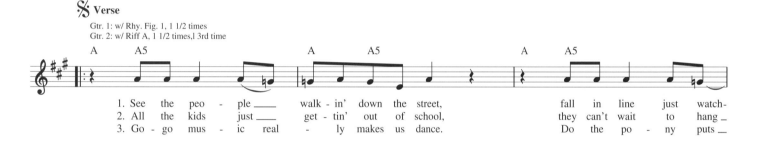

White Wedding

Words and Music by Billy Idol

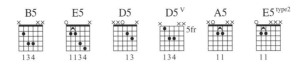

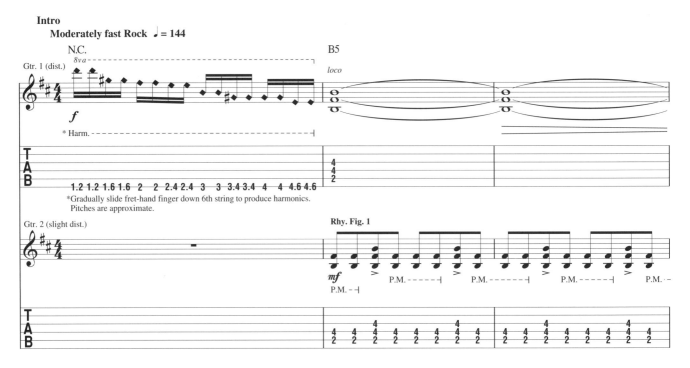

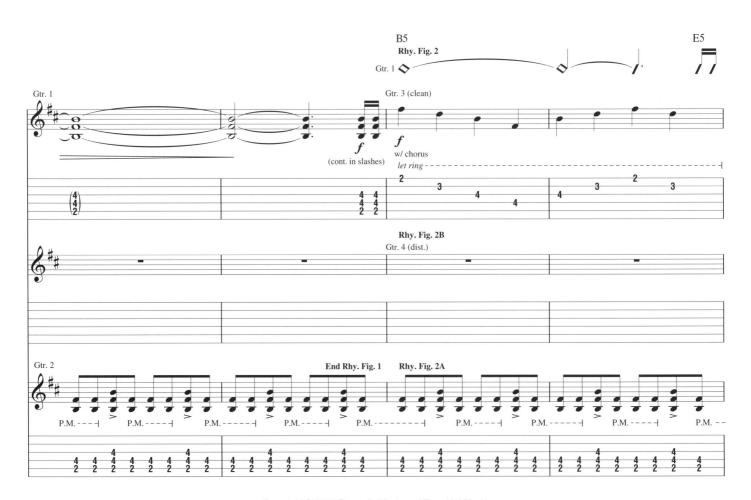

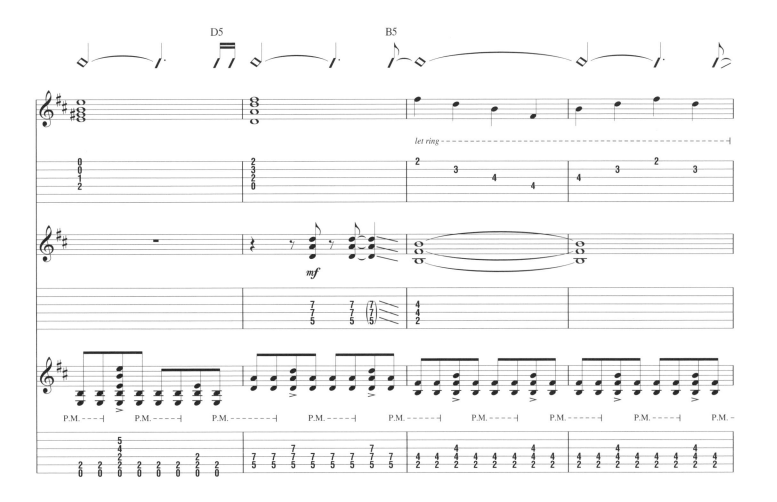

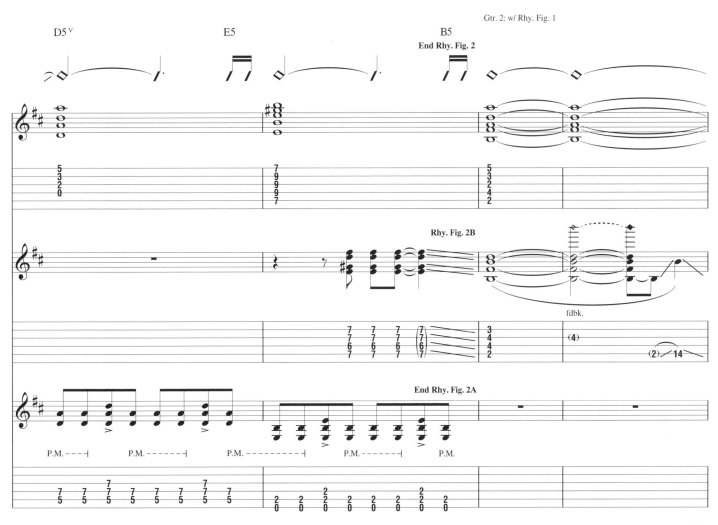

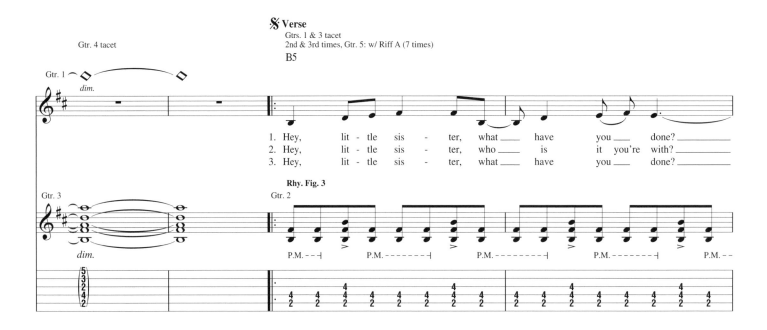

𝄋 Verse

Gtrs. 1 & 3 tacet
2nd & 3rd times, Gtr. 5: w/ Riff A (7 times)

B5

Gtr. 1

dim.

1. Hey, lit - tle sis - ter, what __ have you __ done? _____
2. Hey, lit - tle sis - ter, who __ is it you're with? _____
3. Hey, lit - tle sis - ter, what __ have you __ done? _____

Gtr. 3

Rhy. Fig. 3

Gtr. 2

dim.

P.M. --- ┤   P.M. ------- ┤   P.M. -------- ┤   P.M. ------- ┤   P.M. --

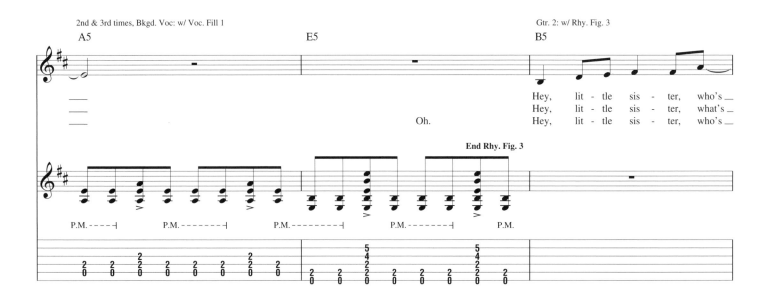

2nd & 3rd times, Bkgd. Voc: w/ Voc. Fill 1   Gtr. 2: w/ Rhy. Fig. 3

A5   E5   B5

___   Hey, lit - tle sis - ter, who's __
___   Hey, lit - tle sis - ter, what's __
___   Oh.   Hey, lit - tle sis - ter, who's __

End Rhy. Fig. 3

P.M. ----- ┤   P.M. ------- ┤   P.M. -------- ┤   P.M. ------- ┤   P.M.

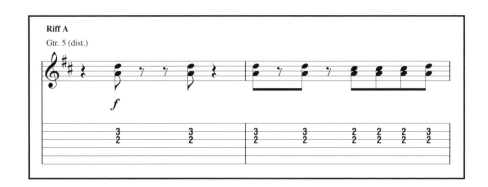

Riff A

Gtr. 5 (dist.)

f

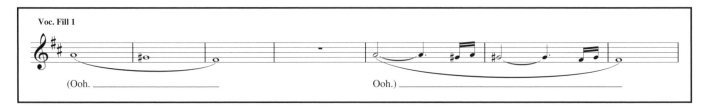

Voc. Fill 1

(Ooh. _____   Ooh.) _____

258

A5   E5

____ the on - ly one? _____
____ your fas - ci - na(tion)? _____
____ the on - ly one? _____

3rd time, Bkgd. Voc.: w/ Voc. Fill 3

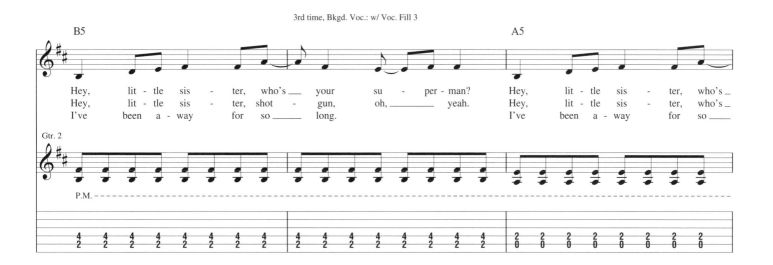

B5   A5

Hey, lit - tle sis - ter, who's ___ your su - per - man? Hey, lit - tle sis - ter, who's _
Hey, lit - tle sis - ter, shot - gun, oh, _____ yeah. Hey, lit - tle sis - ter, who's _
I've been a - way for so _____ long. I've been a - way for so ____

Gtr. 2

P.M. -

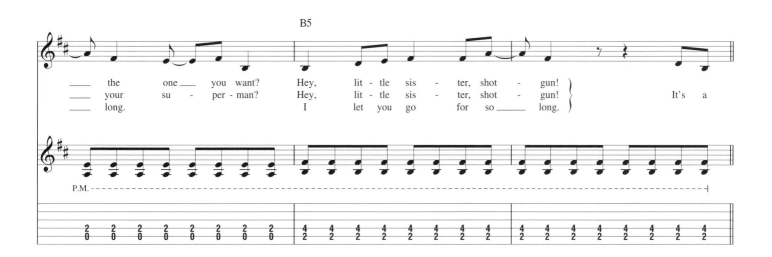

B5

____ the one ___ you want? Hey, lit - tle sis - ter, shot - gun!   It's a
____ your su - per - man? Hey, lit - tle sis - ter, shot - gun!
____ long. I let you go for so _____ long.

P.M. -

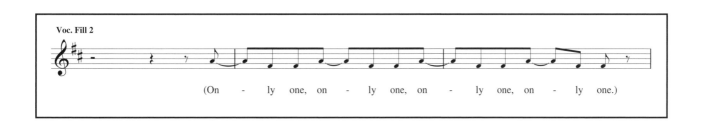

Voc. Fill 2

(On - ly one, on - ly one, on - ly one, on - ly one.)

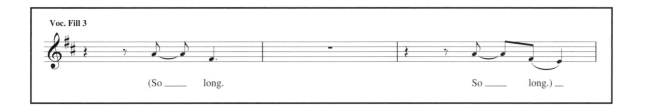

Voc. Fill 3

(So ___ long. So ___ long.)

Chorus

2nd & 3rd times, Gtr. 5: w/ Riff A (4 times)

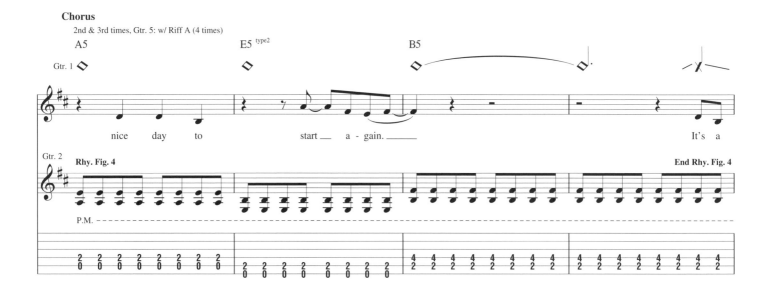

nice day to   start __ a - gain. _____   It's a

To Coda ⊕

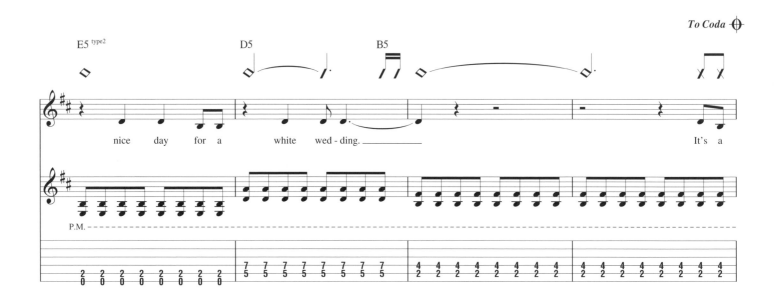

nice day for a   white wed - ding. _____   It's a

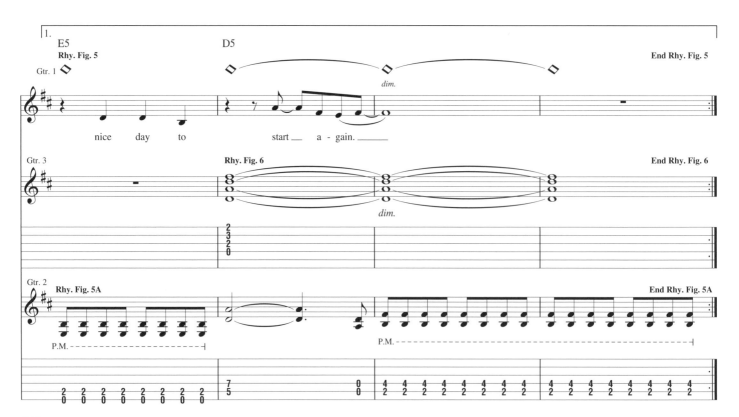

nice day to   start __ a - gain. _____

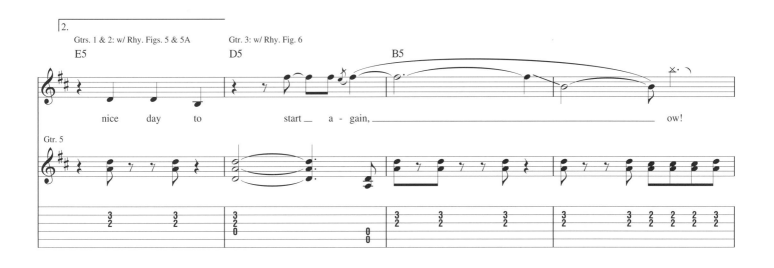

nice day to start a - gain, ow!

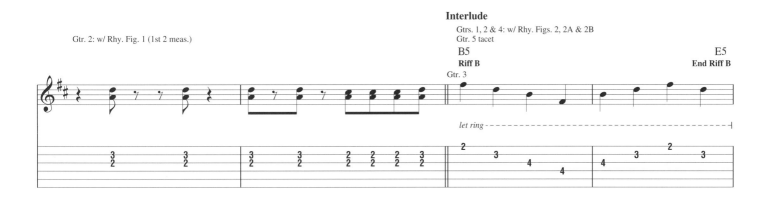

Interlude

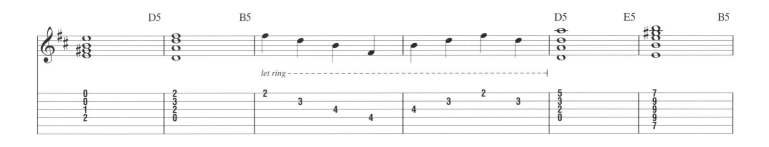

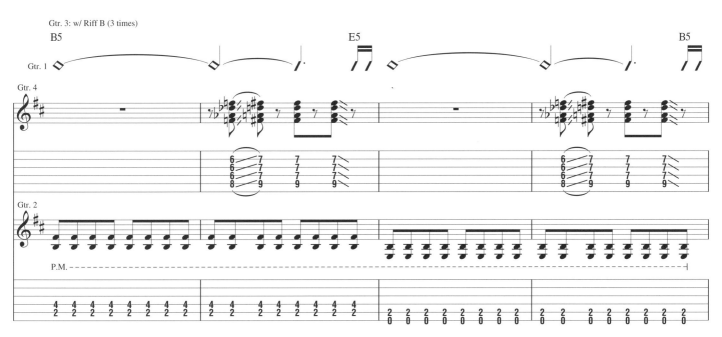

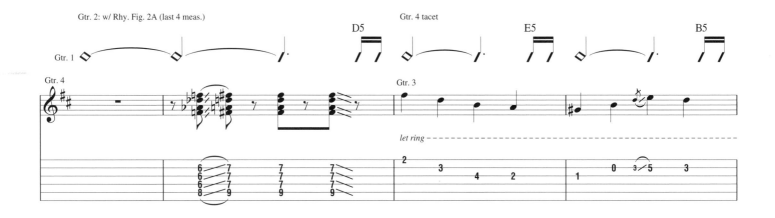

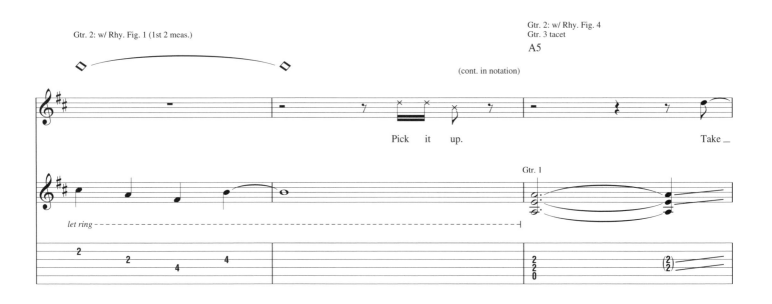

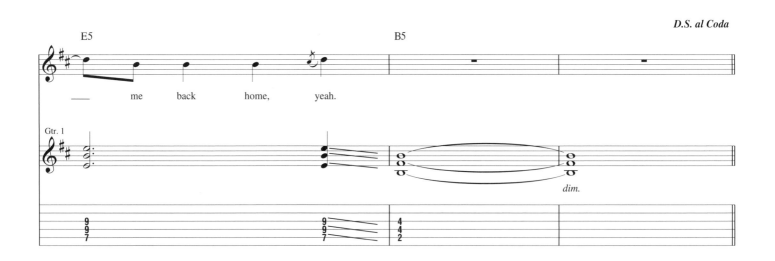

⊕ Coda

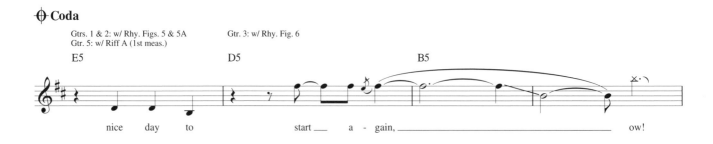

Bridge

Gtr. 2: w/ Rhy. Fig. 5A (last 2 meas.)

Gtr. 2: w/ Rhy. Fig. 1 (3 1/2 times)

B5

There is noth-ing fair ___ in this world, ___ girl. ___

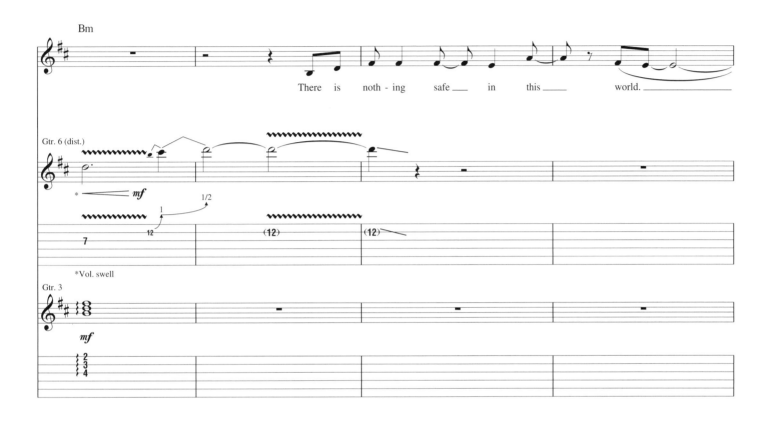

Bm

There is noth-ing safe ___ in this ___ world. ___

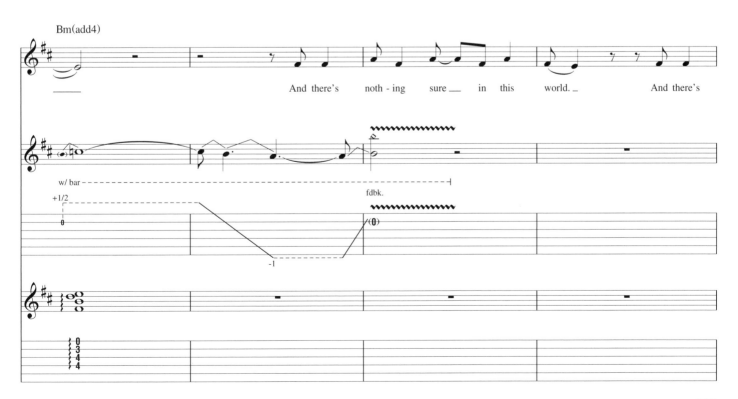

Bm(add4)

And there's noth-ing sure ___ in this world. ___ And there's

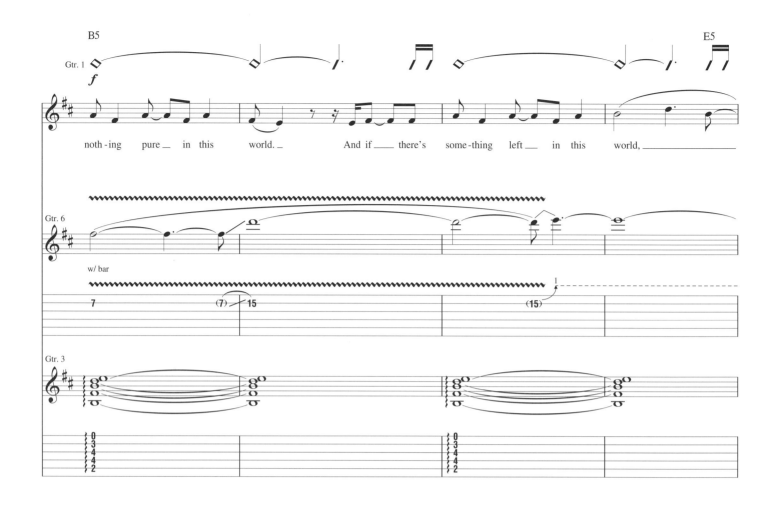

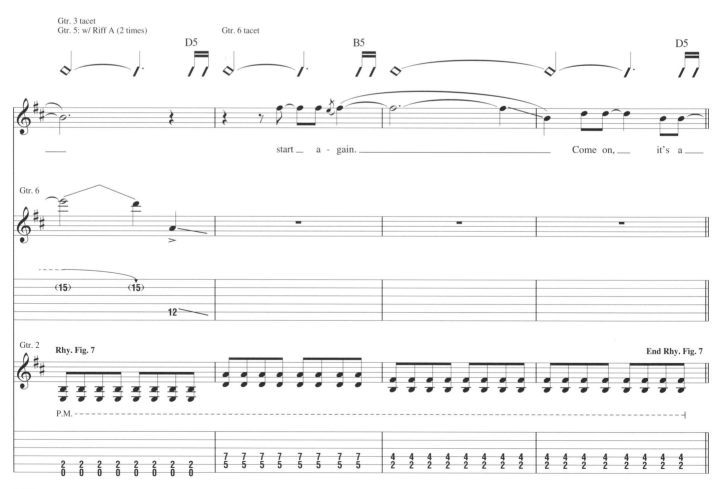

Outro-Chorus

Gtr. 5: w/ Riff A (till fade)

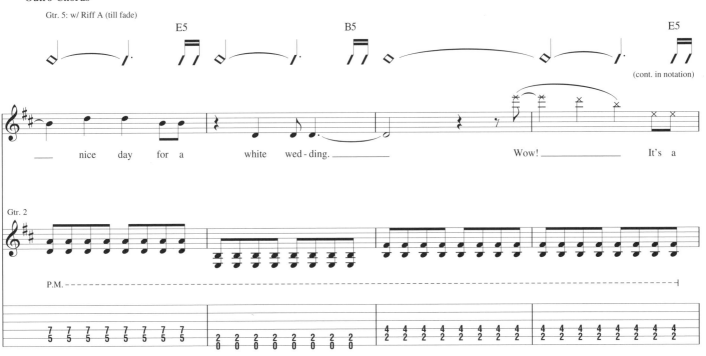

(cont. in notation)

nice day for a   white wed - ding. _____   Wow! _____   It's a

Gtr. 2

P.M.

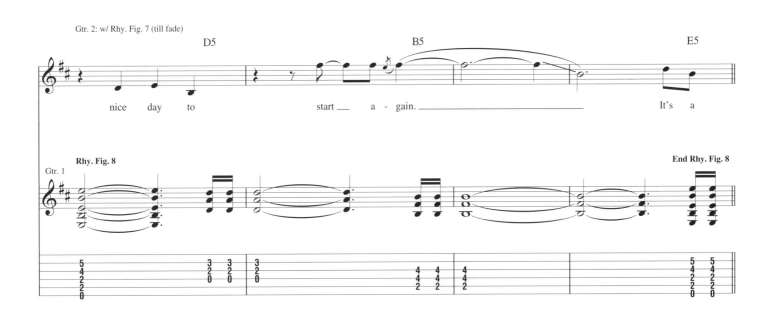

Gtr. 2: w/ Rhy. Fig. 7 (till fade)

nice day to   start ___ a - gain. _____   It's a

Rhy. Fig. 8   **End Rhy. Fig. 8**

Gtr. 1

Repeat and fade

Gtr. 1: w/ Rhy. Fig. 8 (till fade)

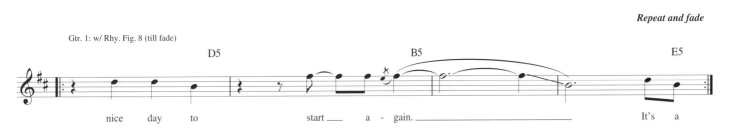

nice day to   start ___ a - gain. _____   It's a

You Oughta Know

Lyrics by Alanis Morissette

Music by Alanis Morissette and Glen Ballard

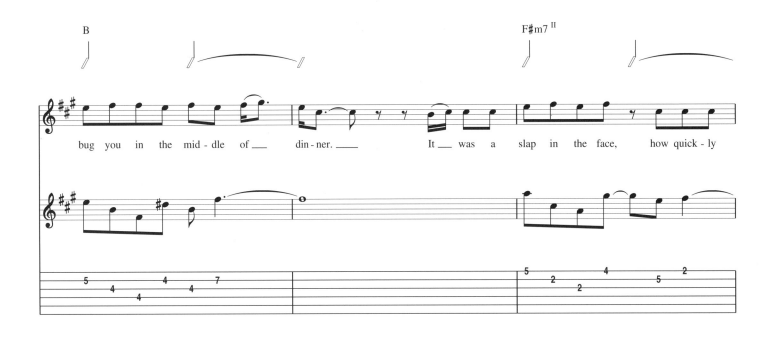

D.S. al Coda 1

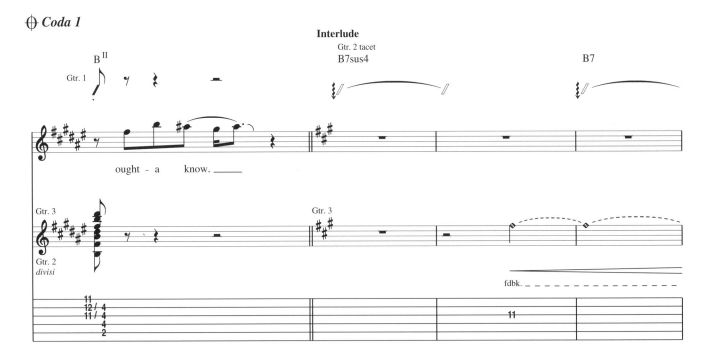

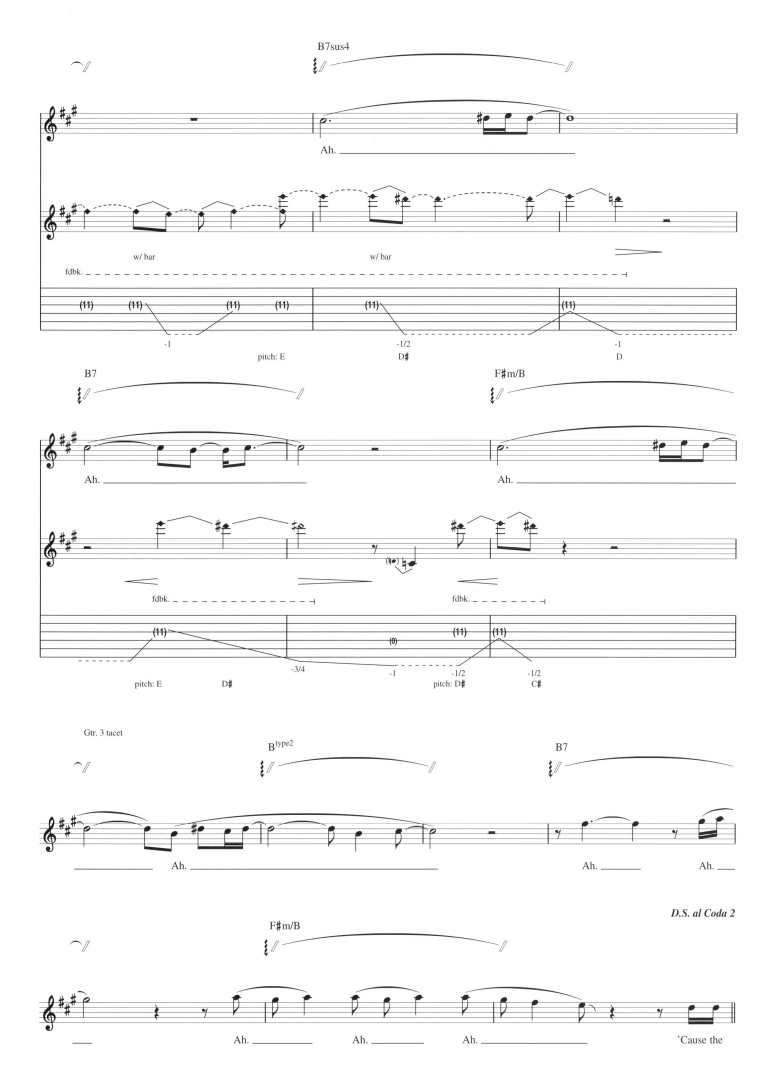

⊕ *Coda 2*

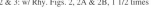

ought - a know. I'm here to re - mind you of the mess

you left when you went a - way. It's not fair to de - ny me of the cross

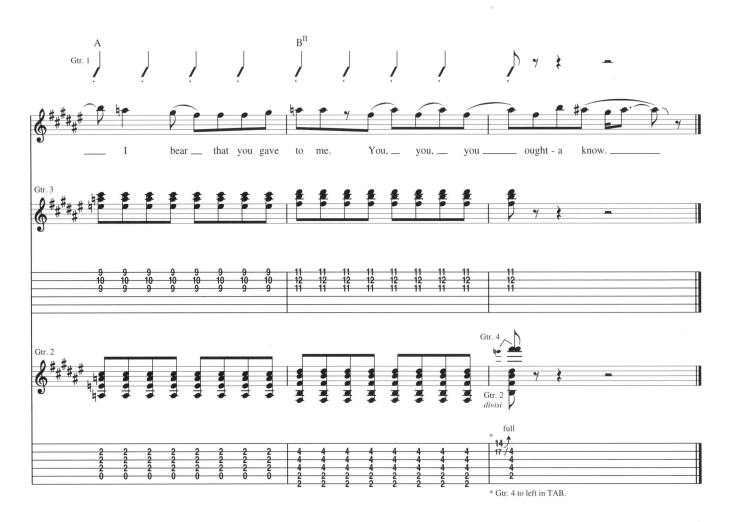

I bear that you gave to me. You, you, you ought - a know.

* Gtr. 4 to left in TAB.

272